Handmade Baby Clothes

An Allen D. Bragdon Book

Distributed by Dodd, Mead & Company New York

Handmade
Baby Clothes

by
Lisbeth Perrone

Designed, Produced, and Published by
Allen D. Bragdon Publishers, Inc.
153 West 82nd Street
New York, NY 10024

Staff for this book:
Editor-in-Chief: Allen D. Bragdon
Editor/Writer: Judith Rubin
Layout: Mindy Lewis
Drawings: Carol Winter
Book Design: John B. Miller
Sewing Consultant: Mary Guay
Proofreader: Evelyn Wheeler
Production Assistants: Hans Schmitt,
Peter Chotin
Photography: Allen Clifford Bragdon
Assistant: Robert MacDonald
Doll models: Marsha Evans Moore
Production/Styling Assistants: Judith
Rubin, Catherine Craemer
Location: The Mohonk Mountain
House, New Paltz, New York
Location Coordination: Faire Hart
Props Contributed by: The Magic
Treehouse, New York City; Faire
Hart, New Paltz, New York;
Mescowitz Graphics, Samsonville,
New York; Christopher Rubacha;
Cecily von Ziegesar, Valentina
Anastasia

Distributed to the retail book trade by
Dodd, Mead & Co.
79 Madison Avenue, New York, N. Y.
10016

Library of Congress Cataloging
in Publication Data

Perrone, Lisbeth.
  Handmade baby clothes.
  "An Allen D. Bragdon book."
  Includes index.
  1. Infants—Clothing. 2. Sewing. 3. Needlework.
I. Title.
TT637.P47 1985   646.4'06   85-14974
ISBN 0-916410-27-7

ISBN 0-916410-27-7

Printed in the U.S.A.

Acknowledgements:
Many skillful hands and minds were involved with this book.
First let me thank Allen D. Bragdon, my publisher, for suggesting that I design
a collection of classic garments for infants combining different needleart techniques. It has been a challenging project, and a joyous experience to deal with
the small dimensions of children on a large scale, and the feelings of their parents.
I would like to thank Judith Rubin for lending her exacting care and creative
imagination to the editing of this book. I am grateful to the following needleartists
for the work they did on various projects—Sara Huntington Brown, Justine Chicks,
Cottontails, Francene Garnett, June Hyne, and Anna Walton.

Lisbeth Perrone
Santa Fe, 1985.

A Word from the Editors

You, the needle-artist, know that it's worth taking the time to make beautiful things by hand. You have, or wish to cultivate in yourself, the patience and skill to crochet a picot edging, knit a flower garden in three colors, appliqué a seascape, embroider a smocked yoke, pleat a tiny pair of pants. Somewhere in your life is a growing infant or not-yet-born baby who will receive and cherish your irreproducible, handmade gift of love.

About difficulty

Classics, with their clean direct lines, tend to be easier to execute than highly decorated designs. Many of the garments are simple enough to be made by a beginner or dispatched swiftly by experienced hands. Take a look, for example at the cross stitch birth sampler at the front of the book, the embroidered pillows in chapter II, the crocheted layette set and the zippered raglan turtleneck pullover in chapter IV. The toys and hangings in chapter V are all quite straightforward too. Other projects are more challenging and intricate. Helpful diagrams and hints for all techniques are in chapter VI. If you need more assistance, consult your local yarn, needlework and crafts shops.

About sizing

The ceremonial dresses in chapter I and the crocheted layette set in chapter IV are sized specifically for newborns. Most of the other garments are in four sizes—6 months, 12 months, 18 months, and 24 months. Sizing is based on average measurements and naturally there will be exceptions. Measure the child if possible before you start a project. Make a guess as to how long the project is likely to take you, and how much the child will grow in that time. A finished garment should be 2-4" larger than the child's actual chest measurement.

When in doubt, make the larger size. The child will grow into it. A new mother frequently finds herself with more gifts of newborn-sized clothing than the baby actually remains newborn-sized long enough to wear.

About materials

We prefer natural fibers and natural fiber blends at all times, for their subtle and brilliant colors, breathability, insulating warmth, durability, and texture. Wool, in particular, remains warm even when it is wet, and is very safe for children's clothing because it will not flame, even when it is dry. Machine washable wools, wool blends, and cottons, soft enough for babies are not a challenge to find.

It is true that acrylics can be machine handled and won't shrink in hot water, but an infant will outgrow a garment so quickly that it won't be washed often, and it is very unlikely that anyone would condemn a hand-sewn gift to the washing machine anyway.

Choose materials and colors that you will enjoy touching and looking at yourself; you will produce finer work. Embroidery, knitting, crochet, appliqué, sewing, and quilting procedures all require constant handling of the materials and close examination of the work for extended periods of time. Eye-easy colors and finger-friendly textures will make a difference.

If you like, why not take the risk of using untraditional colors to make these traditional garments. We suspect that babies are bored by pastels, and if they could talk, they might well scoff at the rigidly defined roles of blue and pink.

Contents

Introduction

With joy and pride, women universally have prepared the clothing and bedding in anticipation of the birth of a child. In the old days they knitted and sewed for utility. But sometimes a woman made the time to create a piece of fancy needlework that would be passed down from one generation to the next.

Traditionally, needlework and sewing have played an important role in a mother's life as practical contributions to the welfare of her baby as well as expressions of her creative feelings. A needlework project was an opportunity for the expectant mother, or often a relative or close friend, to sit down for a while and let her mind wander and rest while still being productive. Through the needlework and cloth there was direct connection between the woman and child; a folkloric bond.

In this day a young working mother's leisure time is precious. She is not likely to take time to sew children's clothes that can be mass produced and bought at low prices. But ceremonial and classic dress-up outfits are different. They are part of a tradition of fine material and loving handwork that people in all walks of life are rediscovering and making part of their contemporary values.

It is a rare joy to work carefully with the finest fabrics and yarns on a tiny scale for a niece, a first grandchild or one's own child-to-be. Perhaps as the world grows more computerized and impersonal we all, again, feel a need to create for those we love. And the satisfaction is as real for a simple linen bib with a touch of decorative embroidery as it is for a nine-piece, crocheted, classic layette set.

In this book you will find complete instructions, patterns and diagrams for many needlework projects, plain and fancy. These are done in cross-stitch, pulled-work, appliqué, smocking, quilting, knitting, crocheting, and tailoring; projects great and small in all the needle arts to warm and honor an infant and its parents.

Lisbeth Perrone
Sante Fe
May 1985

A Simple Embroidered Sampler that an expectant mother might enjoy working on

Cross Stitch Birth Sampler

Babies spend a lot of time in bed. It seems only fair to give them a little reading matter. We imagine that an expectant mother might want to employ her hands to make a birth sampler that will become both a permanent commemoration of her baby's birth and a tiny tapestry. This one is easy enough to be made by an absolute beginner in cross-stitch embroidery. Her baby's eyes might turn to it, as to a familiar friend, and learn the shapes of letters and numbers, literally before you know it. It is the First Word Game; the infant's tabloid. It will, later, perhaps be succeeded by the back of the cereal box. and from there who knows? Acrostics? Jumbles? Financial reports? Even Goethe began by learning the alphabet.

Cross stitch embroidery is slow, soothing employment for the hand, the eye, and the mind. You can finish the sampler off with a row of loops at the top, and hang it on the wall, or you can back it with soft flannel and use it as a small crib blanket.

The finished sampler measures 19½ x 17". Seam allowance is 1½".

Shop for these items
Even weave linen or other fabric, about 18 threads per inch 1 piece 27 x 20", white or desired color.
Fabric for backing (same fabric, muslin, or broadcloth are good for a hanging; soft flannel is good for a coverlet), 1 piece 22½ x 20", white or desired color.
Six-strand embroidery floss, 8 skeins blue or desired color.
Sewing thread to match fabric.
1 embroidery needle.
Graph paper.
Soft pencil.

The border and alphabet
Cut 1 piece of linen 22½ x 20". You should have a 9 x 20" piece left over to make the five loops. A very deep seam allowance of 1½" is included in the measurements. This allows for fraying of the fabric during embroidery, and makes basting unnecessary.

Following the border chart, using 4 strands of embroidery floss, begin at the lower right corner of the fabric and work the border from left to right all around, extending embroidery about 2½" from the edges.

Refer to chapter VI for the charted large alphabet and the numbers. Embroider these in horizontal rows, beginning at the center of each row and working towards the edge and back, then completing the row in the opposite direction.

The newborn's name and birthdate Work out on graph paper your arrangement of words and numbers (child's name and birthdate), using the small alphabet and numbers charts from chapter VI. Each square of the graph paper represents a cross stitch space. Each cross stitch will cover 2 x 2 threads of fabric. Count the number of threads your design will cover, horizontally and vertically, and draw placement outlines on the fabric with a soft pencil.

Cross stitch

Side, center to bottom. (Repeat for other side).

Embroider your design, working from left to right. Draw placement lines on the fabric for the motifs charted on these pages, and embroider them.

Finishing the sampler

To make the sampler into a hanging, cut 5 4 x 9" pieces of linen. Fold in half lengthwise and stitch the long edges together at ½", leaving both ends open. Turn right side out. Fold in half crosswise to make 5 loops. Lay folded loops on right side of embroidered fabric, with raw edges overlapping seam allowance by ½" and folded end of each loop extending toward lower edge. Baste loops to fabric. Place right sides of embroidery and backing together and stitch at 1½", catching edges of loops in stitching, and leaving an opening for turning. Turn right side out and press. Slip-stitch opening closed.

To make sampler into a coverlet, follow the above steps for backing without making loops, using soft flannel as backing fabric. If desired, add a row of edgestitching all around after turning.

The grid lines represent the individual threads of woven fabric. Small squares indicate embroidered stitches. Count threads carefully and work at an even tension to uniformly cover the fabric.

1.

Ceremonial Sets—
each set includes
Dress, Slip,
Bonnet and
Receiving Blanket

Ceremonial Set I

Achristening or baptism is a once-in-a-lifetime occasion, and this ensemble will last generations if it is well-constructed and cared for. Some families make a tradition of embroidering on the back of the dress the names of the children who have worn it.

All the garments in this set, excepting the slip, are plentifully adorned with ribbon and lace. We think the dainty frilly bib and bonnet, both lined with the same fabric, are unusually demure. The bib, which fastens with tiny buttons, covers the bodice in front and extends down the back as well.

The dress is gathered at the yoke, elasticized at the cuffs, and fastens down the back with a zipper. The slip is of a severe, Quakerish simplicity. The blanket is decorated with rows of tucks at top and bottom.

The instructions and measurements are for newborn size, and include ½", ⅜", and ¼" seam allowances. Pink, zig-zag, or overcast to finish exposed seams.

Shop for these items

Fine lightweight cotton fabric, 45" wide, white.
Pre-ruffled eyelet lace trim, 1" wide, white.
⅜" wide ribbon, white.
⅛" to ¼" wide buttons, white mother-of-pearl.
Cotton sewing thread, white.
Single-fold bias tape ½" wide, 1 package, white.
Dressmaker's carbon paper.
Tissue or tracing paper, 18 x 24", 4 sheets (to make paper patterns).
For dress, 1½ yds. fabric.
  7⅓ yds. lace.
  4 yds. ribbon.

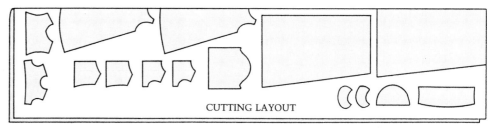

CUTTING LAYOUT

10" of ¼" elastic.
1 12" zipper, white.
1 button.
For slip, 25" fabric.
For bonnet, ¼ yd. fabric.
  45" lace.
  2¼ yds. ribbon.
  Bias tape.
For bib, ¼ yd. fabric.
  48" lace.
  3 yds. ribbon
  26" of ⅝" wide beading lace, white.

2 buttons
Bias tape.
For blanket, 1 yd. fabric.
  4 yds. lace.
  5 yds. ribbon.

Cutting and marking the fabric

Enlarge and trace pattern pieces onto tissue paper. Transfer all markings. Cut out paper pattern pieces and pin to fabric, following the cutting layout. Transfer all markings with dressmaker's carbon and cut out.

DRESS

1. Sew shoulder seams of yokes at ½". Construct 2 and set one aside as lining.

2. Gather upper edges of front and back dress. Attach to front and back yokes with ½" seam allowance. Adjust gathers evenly before stitching. Press seam allowance up toward neck.

3. Sew center back seam at ½", leaving 12" opening unsewn for zipper placement. Press seam open from neck to hem.

4. Sew zipper in center back opening.

5. Collar is constructed with 2 pieces, each having a ¼" seam allowance. Sew lace to outer edges of collars at ¼", leaving neck edges unsewn. With right sides together, construct the collar sections by sewing each collar piece with lace to one without lace at ¼", leaving neck edge open. Notch curves. Turn right side out and press. Machine-baste neck edge.

6. Attach wrong side of collars to the right side of the neck edge at ¼". The lace should meet the center at the ¼" stitching line. Match back collar to back neck edge notch.

7. Turn up the yoke lining piece ¼" along bottom edge front and back stitch; press ½" along center back edge of yoke.

8. Sew yoke lining to neck edge at ¼", following previous line of stitching established in collar application (place right side yoke to right side collar.) Notch seam allowance. Fold yoke lining to inside of body. Press neck edge flat.

Slip-stitch the center back edge of the yoke lining to the center back of the garment. Stitch close to zipper.

On the right side of the dress, stitch ⅛" on yoke front and back, catching yoke lining in this line of stitching.

Machine-baste yoke lining to armhole at ¼".

9. Run gathering threads around sleeve caps. Match notches to armholes and adjust gathers evenly. Stitch at ½". With right sides together, sew lace to sleeve hem at ¼".

Press seam up toward sleeve. On right side, edgestitch close to seam, securing seam allowance in this line of stitching.

Center bias along casing mark: insert 5" of ¼" elastic. Anchor securely at each end within ½" seam allowance.

10. Sew side seams and sleeve seams at ½". Press open.

11. At hem of dress, place right side of lace to right side of hem and sew at ¼". Press seam up toward dress. Right side up, edgestitch close to seam, securing seam allowance in line of stitching.

12. Sew 2 rows of lace (wrong side of lace to right side of dress) at scant ¼" according to pattern markings. Cover the line of stitching by centering the ⅜" ribbon over the raw edge of lace. Slip-stitch by hand or machine edgestitch in place.

13. Sew in 3 rows of ½" tucks along remaining pattern marking lines.

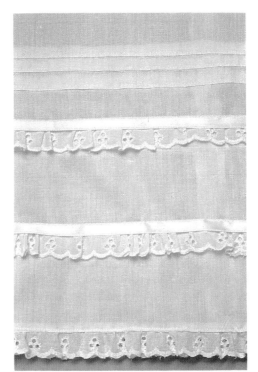

Rows and rows of ruffled lace, ribbon, and tucks create a tiered effect on the skirt of the ceremonial dress (steps 11-13).

The fullness of the skirt is gathered at the underarm and joined to the double-faced yoke (step 2). This join is finished with a row of topstitching along the lower edge of the yoke (step 8). Note the zipper closure (step 4) and the double-faced, lace-edged collar (steps 5 and 6).

BIB

1. Sew shoulder seams for bib and bib lining at ¼". Press seams open.

2. On bib and lining, press center back edge ¼" to inside.

3. Thread ⅜" ribbon through beading lace. Center over markings on bib only. Edgestitch in place.

4. Attach lace to bib only at ¼" from outer edge. Do not join any lace at center back or at neck edge.

5. With right sides together, join bib and lining, with ¼" seam allowances. Do not sew center back seam. Seam all other edges, including neck edge.

6. Clip neck edge, and trim corners diagonally. Turn bib right side out and press.

7. With seam allowances folded inside, edgestitch center back seam closed.

8. Sew on buttons and make buttonholes as pattern markings indicate.

9. Cut 4 16" pieces of ribbon, and tack to outer corners of bib as ties.

The bib's outer edges are finished with ruffled eyeletting (step 4). The bib surface is decorated with two applied strips of beading lace, through which ribbons are threaded (step 3). Like the bonnet, the bib is lined with the same fabric used for its exterior (steps 1, 2 & 5).

BONNET

1. Sew lining brim to lining back at ¼". Notch seam allowance. Set aside.

2. Bonnet exterior: Sew lace to bonnet brim front edge, matching right sides and stitching at ¼".

3. Attach second row of lace over center marking line on bonnet brim, stitching in place at scant ¼". Cover raw edge of lace with ribbon, hand slip-stitched or machine-stitched in place.

4. Sandwich lace in the ¼" seam allowance of the bonnet trim joining to the bonnet back. Notch seam allowance.

5. On right side of bonnet, hand slip-stitch or machine edgestitch ribbon at seamline.

6. Place bonnet and bonnet lining with right sides together and stitch at ¼" all around, leaving a small center back opening. Clip corners diagonally.

7. Turn bonnet right side out and press. Sew up center back opening at ¼".

8. Attach ½" bias to bottom edge of bottom lining to form casing for ribbon. Turn ends of bias back in for finishing, but do not stitch end openings closed. Edgestitch casing.

9. Insert a 36" piece of ⅜" wide ribbon through casing for bonnet tie.

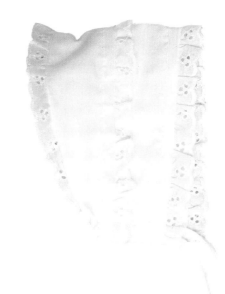

Eyelet lace trim fans outward from the edges of the bonnet back (step 4). The ribbon tie is enclosed in a casing around the lower edge, making the bonnet comfortably adjustable (steps 8 and 9).

Note the direction of the lace applications on the bonnet. The front lace edge extends forward to frame the face. The back lace edge is perpendicular to the sides of the bonnet. See steps 2-4. The bonnet is fully lined with the same fabric used to make the exterior (steps 1 and 6).

SLIP

1. Sew shoulder seams at ⅜".

2. Sew side seams at ⅜".

3. Finish hem, neck, and armhole edges with narrow hems by folding under ⅛" twice. Stitch in place.

BLANKET

1. Cut a piece of 45" wide fabric to measure 32" long.

2. Using the length of the piece, make 3 ½" tucks 7" from the ends. You will use 6" of fabric to do this, shortening the width to 39".

3. With wrong sides of lace and fabric together, sew lace to edge with ¼" seam allowance at ¼", mitering lace at corners. Press seam allowances away from lace edge.

4. Cover and enclose the seam allowance with ribbon, hand slip-stitching or machine edgestitching both edges. Miter ribbon at corners.

5. Make bows of ribbon and hand-tack at corners.

Two sets of tucks are made and stitched down across the breadth of the blanket (step 2). Like other garments in this set, the blanket is lavishly finished with ribbon and lace around the edges (steps 3-5).

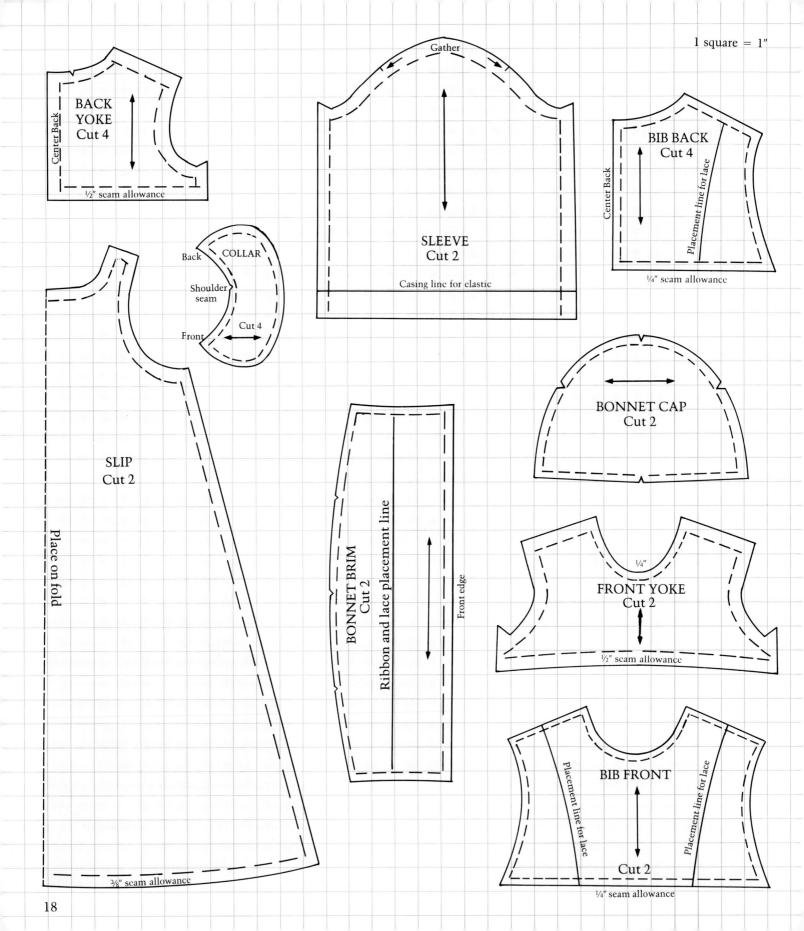

1 square = 1"

BACK
YOKE
Cut 4

Center Back

½" seam allowance

SLEEVE
Cut 2

Gather

Casing line for elastic

BIB BACK
Cut 4

Center Back

Placement line for lace

¼" seam allowance

COLLAR

Back

Shoulder
seam

Front

Cut 4

BONNET CAP
Cut 2

SLIP
Cut 2

Place on fold

⅜" seam allowance

BONNET BRIM
Cut 2

Ribbon and lace placement line

Front edge

FRONT YOKE
Cut 2

¼"

½" seam allowance

BIB FRONT

Placement line for lace

Placement line for lace

Cut 2

¼" seam allowance

18

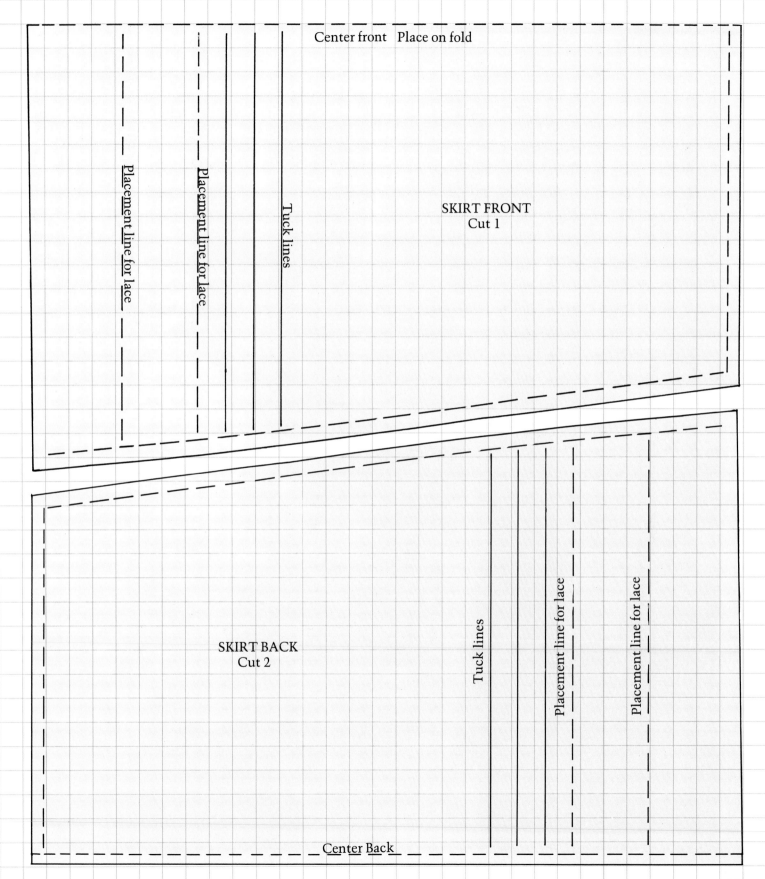

Center front   Place on fold

Placement line for lace

Placement line for lace

Tuck lines

SKIRT FRONT
Cut 1

SKIRT BACK
Cut 2

Tuck lines

Placement line for lace

Placement line for lace

Center Back

Ceremonial Set II

This dress of fine cotton sateen expresses in its design a formal sweetness. Every detail communicates the love and care surrounding the precious infant. It is gathered in tiny tucks across the back and front yokes, and in soft folds at the shoulders and wrists. It is joined simply at the back of the neck with a tiny thread-loop closure and a mother-of-pearl button.

A row of hearts, embroidered in cross stitch down the dress front, adds a sense of subdued festivity, appropriate to the ceremony of christening or baptism.

To make this dress the centerpiece of an entire ceremonial ensemble, use the patterns from Ceremonial Set I. With the same cotton sateen, sew a matching bib, bonnet, receiving blanket, and slip.

Measurements and instructions are for newborn size and include ⅝", ⅜", ½" and ¼" seam allowances. Pink, zig-zag, or overcast to finish exposed seams.

Shop for these items

Fabric: Cotton sateen or other fine cotton, 45" wide, white.
Lace: Pre-ruffled eyelet trim, 1" wide, white.
Ribbon: ⅜" wide, white.
Buttons: ⅛" to ¼" wide, mother-of-pearl.
Cotton sewing thread, white.
4 sheets of 18 x 24" tissue or tracing paper (to make paper pattern).
Dressmaker's carbon paper.
For dress, 1½ yds. fabric.
   1 button.
   1 package of single-fold white bias tape.
   20" of ½" wide elastic.
   Six-strand embroidery floss, 1 skein blue or desired color.
   Waste canvas, 1 piece 10 x 2" (for embroidery).

   1 embroidery needle.
   Tweezers.
For slip, 25" or 45" wide lightweight cotton fabric.
For bonnet, ¼ yd. fabric.
   45" lace.
   2¼ yds. ribbon.
For bib, ¼ yd fabric.
   48" lace.
   3 yds. ribbon.
   26" of ⅜" wide beading lace, white.
   2 buttons.
For blanket, 1 yd. fabric.
   4 yds. lace.
   5 yds. ribbon.

Cutting and marking the fabric

Enlarge pattern pieces and trace onto tissue paper. Transfer all markings. Cut out paper pattern and pin to fabric, following the cutting layout. With dressmaker's carbon, transfer all pattern markings to fabric and cut out all pieces except front.

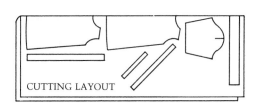

CUTTING LAYOUT

DRESS

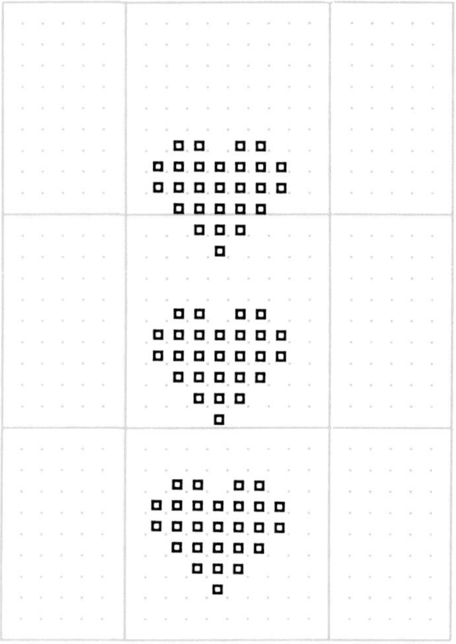

3. To bias bind the neck edge and center back opening, stitch the neck bias at ¼" to the neck edge of garment with right sides together. Start and finish bias at point marked on the back neck edge. Clip seam allowances. Press seam up against binding. Turn in ¼" hem on bias binding. Press. Turn binding to inside. Encase raw neck edges, and slip-stitch pressed edge over seam allowance.

4. Sleeves. Gather upper edge of sleeve between notches (stitch first line at ¼", second line at ⅝"). To hem sleeve, turn bottom edge under ¼", then turn in again ¼". Stitch.

Prepare the casing by pressing edges under ¼". Apply casing where marked on sleeve, stitching along sewing line. Insert a 5½" piece of elastic in casing. Baste securely across ends of elastic, overlapping at seam lines ¼" to hold in place. Elastic should finish at 5".

5. With right sides together, and matching sleeve center to shoulder seam, adjust gathers in sleeve cap evenly. Sew in sleeve at ⅝".

6. Stitch at ⅝" one continuous seam from hem of sleeve to bottom hem of dress. Hand-tack seam allowances open at lower edge of sleeve hem.

7. Sew ends of piping together at ⅝". Open seam allowances. Attach right sides together at ⅝" to bottom edge of dress. Match side seams, center front, and center back. Press side seam allowances towards hem.

8. With right sides together, sew the 2 pieces of the ruffle together at both ends. Press seam allowances open. Hem the ruffle along one edge by pressing up ¼", folding back ¼" again and stitching to the wrong side. Gather ruffle along ⅝" seam line to create fullness. Attach ruffle to piping at ⅝", with right sides together, matching side seams, center front, and center back, adjusting others evenly throughout. Stitch. Press seam allowances up toward dress. With right side of dress facing, stitch in the indentation created by the joining of the piping to the dress, catching the seam allowances of the ruffle and the piping in this line of stitching. This is called "channel stitching." Continue channel stitching completely around the dress.

9. Finishing. Sew button to right back neck binding as per markings. Make a thread loop in left back end of neck binding large enough for the button to go through. Work blanket stitch tightly along the full length of the loop.

SLIP, BIB, BONNET, AND BLANKET

Use the same fabric for bib, bonnet and blanket as you used for the dress. Use 25" of 45" lightweight cotton for the slip. You will also need ribbon, lace, and beading lace as specified. Follow instructions for making slip, bib, bonnet, and blanket in Ceremonial Set I.

Embroidering the front

Baste the waste canvas securely to the wrong side of the front behind the embroidery placement markings. Find the center of the charted heart. Begin the embroidery at the center of the fabric, working each row from right to left towards the edge of the design, and from left to right to finish the cross. Work each stitch through both the fabric and the canvas. All bottom stitches should slant in one direction and all top stitches in the other direction. When the embroidery is complete, wet the waste canvas and remove the threads of canvas with tweezers.

Putting the pieces together

1. Cut out front of dress. Make tucks in front. On right side, fold along tuck lines. Stitch ⅛" from folds, ending stitching opposite dots. Press away from center. Baste around neck edge to hold tucks down. Make tucks in back same as in front. To make center back opening, slash partway down center back as pattern indicates.

2. Sew shoulder seams at ⅝".

A handmade bias band encloses the neck edge and the tiny tucks of the front and back yokes (step 3). Before the tucks are folded (step 1) the neckline has a "stepped" edge, which tucking rounds into a curve. The cross-stitch hearts are embroidered before cutting out the dress front.

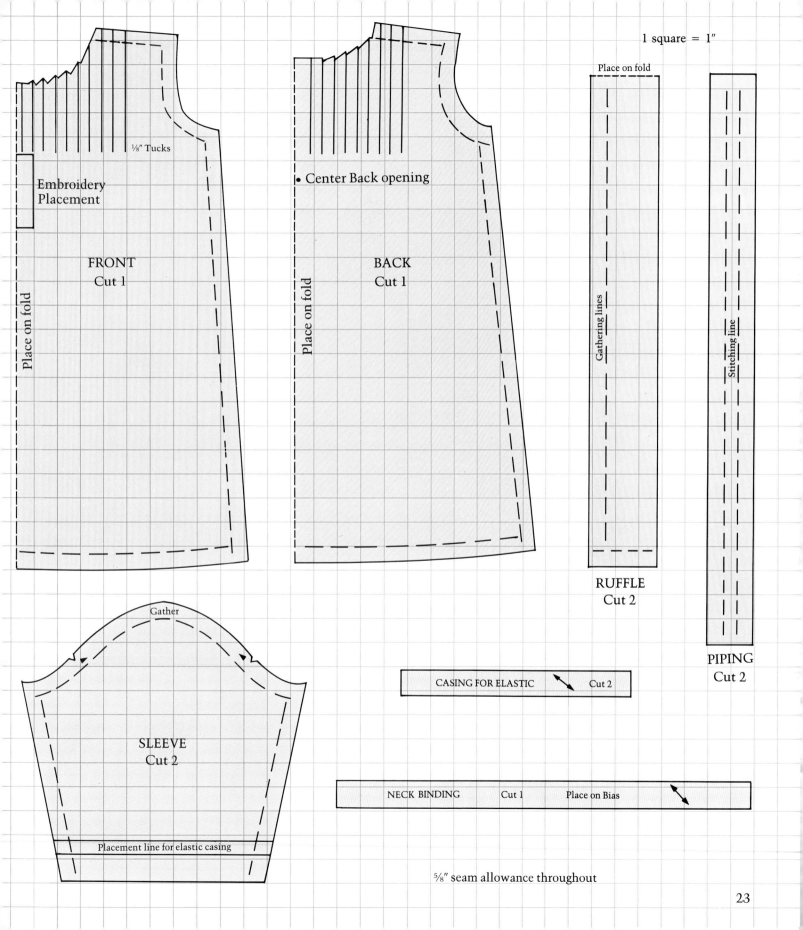

1 square = 1"

¹/₈" Tucks

Embroidery
Placement

Place on fold

FRONT
Cut 1

• Center Back opening

Place on fold

BACK
Cut 1

Place on fold

Gathering lines

RUFFLE
Cut 2

Stitching line

PIPING
Cut 2

Gather

SLEEVE
Cut 2

Placement line for elastic casing

CASING FOR ELASTIC   Cut 2

NECK BINDING   Cut 1   Place on Bias

⅝" seam allowance throughout

23

2.

*Bibs, Pillows
and Quilts*

Three Bibs

Seascape Appliqué
Embroidered Ducks
Pulled-thread Bib
with Matching Bolster

As babies are not born tidy, a practical, washable bib is indispensable as a mealtime clothes-saver. But on special occasions, and at family gatherings, a bib should be every bit as pretty and festive as the rest of the baby's holiday outfit.

Each of the three bibs pictured here is a precious sample of fine stitchery. Since bibs are small, they are good opportunities to learn new techniques—decorative embroidery stitches, appliqué, and pulled-thread work. A bib requires so little fabric that it can be the very finest quality without becoming prohibitively expensive. The value of the gift lies in the giver's loving handwork.

Since bibs suffer so little abrasive wear, and are forgiving in their fit, they can be used frequently and still passed down through the family for another child to wear. For many adults, the pattern and designs on a bib form one of their earliest visual memories of childhood. If you are making one for your own child, you may want to match the colors with a best dress-up outfit.

SEASCAPE APPLIQUÉ

This restful picture of sea and sky, sailboat and gulls is executed in blue and yellow matte fabric with glossy blue and yellow embroidered details. The scalloped edges are meticulously finished with blanket stitch, framing the picture in blue.

The bib is embroidered with satin stitch, stem stitch, and blanket stitch. Finished bib measures 8 x 10".

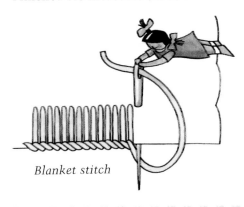

Blanket stitch

Shop for these items
1 11 x 14" piece of lightweight close-woven linen or cotton fabric, white or other background color.
Fabric scraps for appliqué, yellow and light blue.
Six-strand embroidery floss, 1 skein each yellow and light blue.

Cotton sewing thread to match fabric.
24" of ⅜" cotton twill tape.
Dressmaker's carbon paper.
Tracing paper, 11 x 14".
Water-soluble pen for marking fabric.
Embroidery hoop.

Marking the fabric
Trace the actual-size design from these pages onto tracing paper, adding ⅛" all around the shape of the boat and its sail. With dressmaker's carbon, transfer the design to fabrics. Go over all the lines with water-soluble pen, to prevent the lines from fading before you finish the embroidery. The bib itself is not cut out until the appliqué and all embroidery, except for edging, is completed.

The birds and waves
All embroidery is done with two strands of embroidery floss. Carefully cut out the shape of the large bird (yellow fabric). Without turning edges under, baste in position. Place in embroidery hoop, and, with a small, close satin stitch embroi-

der blue outlines and yellow beak and claws. Embroider the smaller background birds with blue satin stitch wings and yellow satin stitch bodies. Embroider the waves in blue stem stitch. Remove basting stitches.

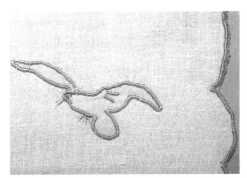

Here's a close-up view of the large gull and the scalloped bib edge. The satin stitch outlines and details are worked in a satin stitch so tiny and close that the stitches build up into a little ridge on the fabric surface.

The boat

Carefully cut out the shapes for the boat (blue fabric) and its sail (yellow fabric). Turn edges under ⅛" and baste pieces in position on background fabric, using small running stitches to hold the edges down.
Note: The small blue boat piece may be optionally embroidered with long satin stitches, instead of appliquéd.

With the sewing thread, work blanket stitch along the side edges of the sail, and all around the boat. With a small, close yellow satin stitch, finish the top and bottom edges of the sail, and embroider the mast. Remove basting stitches.

Edging and finishing

Cut out bib. Without the embroidery hoop, work around the entire scalloped outer edge closely in blanket stitch, using blue floss. Cut the twill tape in half to make two 12" ties. Sew ends securely to opposite sides of the neck opening.

Very small blanket stitches made with sewing thread join the boat and the vertical edges of its sail to the bib. The top and bottom edges of the sail and the mast are done in satin stitch. Appliqué requires patience and care.

Three ducks in a pond, two of them floating, one splashing, are embroidered in split stitch, satin stitch, blanket stitch, and French knots and finished with white piping around the edge. This bib is the simplest and fastest to make of the three.

Embroidery stitches used: Split stitch, satin stitch, lazy daisy stitch, blanket stitch, French knots. Finished bib measures 9 x 12½". All measurements include ½" seam allowance for bib panels, ¼" allowance for ties.

Shop for these items

½ yd. cotton fabric, blue or other background color.
50" pre-made bias piping, white or desired color.
Six-strand embroidery floss, 1 skein white or desired color.
Cotton sewing thread to match.
Dressmaker's carbon paper.
Tracing paper.
Embroidery hoop.

EMBROIDERED DUCKS

Cutting and marking the fabric

Cut along the straight grain of the fabric 2 10 x 13½" pieces for front and back panels, and 2 1½ x 18" strips for ties.

Trace the pattern for the embroidered ducks, the rounded top edge, and the rounded lower corners of the bib onto tracing paper. With dressmaker's carbon, transfer duck design to one bib panel. Transfer edge and corner markings to both bib panels.

Embroidering the design

Note: Baste the edges of the fabric to prevent fraying. Use an embroidery hoop and three strands of embroidery floss.

Outline the ducks with split stitch. Fill in the duck eyes and duck bills with satin stitch. Use lazy daisy stitch for the drops of water .

Embroider the small waves of the duckpond surface with an open, irregular blanket stitch, and place French knots between the vertical lines of the blanket stitch.

Putting the pieces together

Fold the 2 strips of fabric you cut to make the ties vertically in half and press. Stitch edges together with ¼" seam allowance, tapering one end to a point and leaving other end open for turning. Turn strips right side out and press.

Machine-baste the piping around the right side of the front panel with the folded edge of the piping facing in, and the piping seamline on the ½" seam allowance of the fabric. Baste the unfinished ends of the ties in position over the piping on either side of the neck opening. Position the back panel over the piping, matching edges of fabric with right sides together. Pin the ties out of the way, and stitch around bib, leaving a 2" opening on one edge for turning. Turn bib right side out. Hand-stitch opening. Press.

The fragile delicacy of pulled-thread embroidery, fully backed by solid muslin, makes this bib the most elegant of the group. It is also accompanied by instructions for a matching ruffled bolster.

Pulled-thread work is done on even weave fabric. Each stitch is pulled tightly, grouping some threads of the fabric together and separating others, creating an openwork lace effect. We used a thread that matched the fabric color almost exactly, to give a subtle textural contrast.

The pulled-thread set uses four-sided stitch and satin stitch. The finished bib measures 10" square. The finished bolster measures 11" long and 10" around. The seam allowance is 1½".

Shop for these items

Coarse, even weave linen or other fabric, about 12 threads per inch, off-white or desired color.
For bib only, 1 piece 13 x 13".
For bolster only. 1 piece 13 x 14".

PULLED-THREAD BIB

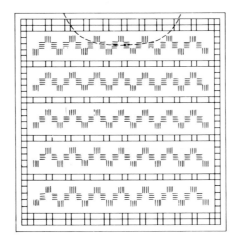

For both bib and bolster, ½ yd or one piece 14 x 18".
Fabric of firmer weave for lining, interlining, and end pieces (broadcloth is good).
For bib only, 1 piece 13 x 13".

For bolster only, 1 piece 13 x 20" (if you use a prefabricated bolster you don't need interlining, one 6 x 9" piece for the ends is sufficient).
For both bib and bolster, ½ yd.
24" of pre-ruffled eyelet trim, 2½" wide (for bolster only).
Mercerized cotton size 5, 1 1¾ oz. (50 gr.) ball, or 6 small skeins for each piece, off-white or color to match or nearly match fabric.
Cotton sewing thread to match fabric.
Polyester fiberfill or prefabricated bolster, 11" long and 10" around (for bolster only).
1 yd. twill tape, ¼" wide (for bib ties).
1 embroidery needle.
Tracing paper.

Cutting and marking the fabric

Measurements include a very deep seam allowance of 1½". This allows for fraying of the edges during embroidery, and makes basting unnecessary.

Cut two 13 x 13″ pieces of fabric, one of the linen and one of the interlining material. Trace the actual-size curve of the neck edge from these pages onto tracing paper, and transfer it to one edge of each piece of fabric with dressmaker's carbon.

Pulled-thread embroidery—give each stitch a tug. Don't use an embroidery hoop.

Embroidering the bib

Use a single strand of size 5 mercerized cotton for the four-sided stitch and a double strand for the satin stitch. To maintain consistent tension, always work a stitch in the same direction. Satin stitch can be worked either from right to left, or from left to right. Four-sided stitch can be worked either horizontally or vertically. Work in the direction most comfortable to you. To make rows of stitches symmetrical, begin each row at center of fabric and work towards the edge. Turn work around so that you can embroider your stitches in the same di-

Marking center of fabric

rection, and work from the center towards the opposite edge to mirror the first half.

Mark center of fabric. Following the embroidery chart, you can either work the border of a single row of four-sided stitches first, and then fill in the horizontal alternating rows of satin stitch and four-sided stitch, or work the horizontal rows first and surround them with the border. Embroidery should extend to about ½″ from the seam allowance (2″ from raw edge). There should be

3 threads separating each four-sided stitch row from each satin stitch row.

Putting the bib together

Cut the twill tape in half to make 2 18″ bib ties. Pin the right sides of bib and lining together, matching edges and basting the ties in position between the layers of fabric. Stitch 1½″ from edge, leaving a 2″ opening along one edge for turning. Clip and trim seams about ½″. Turn bib right side out. Hand stitch opening closed. Press lightly.

PULLED-THREAD BOLSTER

 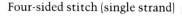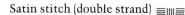
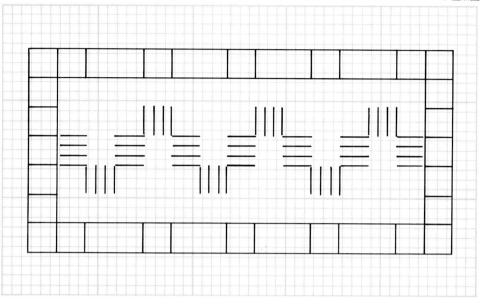

Use the same materials and embroidery stitches as you used for the bib. The finished bolster measures 11″ long and 10″ around.

Cutting and embroidering

Cut 2 13 x 14″ pieces of fabric, one of the linen and one of the interlining material. You need a strip 6 x 9″ left over for the end pieces. Embroider the linen in the same manner as the bib (see bib instructions).

Joining the ruffle and lining

Pin the eyelet ruffle on right side of linen along the 2 side edges, right side down, with the ruffled edge facing in and the other edge of ruffle extending slightly past the seam allowance. Machine-baste along seam allowance. Turn seam allowance under and press so that ruffle extends outward from fabric edge. Turn the unruffled edges of the linen, and all four edges of the lining fabric, under 1½″ and press. Place linen and interlining together with right sides out, and machine-stitch on right side of linen close to edge of fabric. (If you have no interlining, follow this step without it.) Remove basting threads.

Hand-stitch the unruffled edges together to form a cylinder and stuff. Fold ends of ruffle around each other and hand-stitch.

Making and joining the end pieces

Trace the semicircle and its seam allowance from these pages onto tracing paper. Transfer to folded fabric for end pieces. Cut out. Clip and turn edges under ½″. Machine-stitch close to edge. Hand-stitch circles to each end.

Squares and rectangles represent four-sided stitch. Parallel lines indicate satin stitch. Blue lines represent the threads of the woven fabric. Black lines indicate the embroidered stitches. Note that the horizontal rows of four-sided stitch are made up of short stitches that wrap around three threads of fabric, and long stitches that wrap around six threads. The vertical stitches are all short, while the horizontal stitches are alternately long and short, with two short stitches at each end. The vertical rows of four-sided stitch that run along the side edges are comprised only of short stitches.

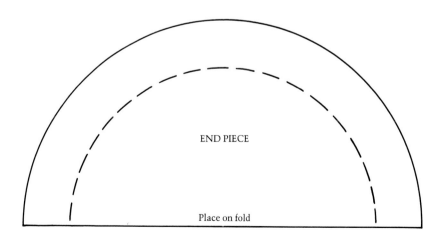

END PIECE

Place on fold

Pillows and Bolsters

Embroidered Pillows

Ruffled bolster with blue geometric design

Ruffled bolster with white floral design

Heart-shaped pillow with green floral grid

Square pillow with pink and green cross stitch flowers

The following bolsters and pillows are decorated with either cross stitch or pulled-thread embroidery on even weave linen or other fabric. Even weave fabric has the same number of threads per inch lengthwise as crosswise. The weave of the fabric must be fairly coarse, so that the threads can be counted precisely in order to duplicate the design. You need only to know or learn four of the easiest embroidery stitches—satin stitch, four-sided stitch, cross stitch, and back stitch.

Stuff pillows and bolsters either with loose stuffing, such as fiberfill, or with prefabricated foam shapes. A pulled-thread pillow must be interlined to prevent the stuffing from showing or escaping through the holes, if loose stuffing is used.

Interlinings, backings, and side pieces should be made with material of firmer weave. We used muslin or broadcloth in colors to match the linen. Fabrics of different colors or finishes will produce different effects. Openwork can be emphasized by lining the embroidery with a darker color. The side pieces of a bolster or the backing of a pillow can be made of shiny woven silk or satin that picks up the color in the embroidery yarns.

You may want to re-arrange or modify some of the embroidered designs. Sketching any changes or new ideas on a sheet of graph paper will help to clarify them. Choose fabric and yarn colors that suit your own tastes and the decor of the baby's room.

Please refer to chapter VII for diagrams of embroidery stitches and other supplementary information.

GEOMETRIC BOLSTER

Bolster is embroidered with four-sided stitch and satin stitch. Finished bolster measures 12" long and 10" in circumference.

Shop for these items

Even weave linen or other fabric, about 18 threads per inch, 1 piece 15 x 13" pink or desired color.

Fabric of similar or firmer weave than the linen (broadcloth is good), for interlining and end pieces, 1 piece 22 x 13", or ½ yd (if you are stuffing with a prefabricated insert, interlining is optional and you will need only one 7 x 10" piece for the bolster ends).

24" of pre-ruffled eyelet trim, 2½" wide.

Six-strand embroidery floss, 1 skein each dark blue and light blue, or desired colors.

Mercerized cotton, size 8, 1 skein white or desired color.

Cotton sewing thread to match fabrics.

Polyester fiberfill, or prefabricated bolster, 12" long and 10" around.

1 embroidery needle.

Tracing paper.

Pulled-thread embroidery—give each stitch a tug. Don't use an embroidery hoop.

Cutting and embroidering

Measurements include a very deep seam allowance of 1½". This allows for fraying of the edges during embroidery, and makes basting unnecessary.

Use a single strand of size 8 mercerized cotton for the four-sided stitch and 2 strands of embroidery floss for the satin stitch. Satin stitch should be worked consistently either from left to right, or from right to left. Four-sided stitch can be worked either horizontally or vertically. Work in the manner most comfortable to you. Give each stitch, particularly the four-sided stitch, a tug to group and separate the threads of fabric and create an openwork effect.

Cut 2 15 x 13" pieces of fabric, one of the linen and one of the interlining material. You need a 7 x 10" strip left over for the end pieces.

Following the embroidery chart, establish the framework of four-sided stitches first, making a double row of squares along the two side edges. Work an open-cornered square of satin stitch just inside each square of four-sided stitch. Alternate light blue squares with dark blue squares. Embroider a little rectangle of 5 satin stitches at the center of each square. Alternate light blue centers with dark blue centers.

Joining the ruffle and lining

Pin the eyelet ruffle to right side of linen along the 2 side edges, right side down, with the ruffled edge facing in and the other edge of the ruffle extending slightly past the seam allowance. Machine-baste along seam allowance. Turn seam allowance under and press so that ruffle extends outward from fabric edge. Turn the unruffled edges of the linen, and all four edges of the interlining, under 1½" and press. Place linen and interlining together with right sides out, and machine-stitch close to edge of fabric (if you have no interlining, follow this step without it). Remove basting threads.

Hand-stitch the unruffled edges together to form a cylinder and stuff. Fold ends of ruffle around each other and hand-stitch.

Making and joining the end pieces

Trace the semicircle and its seam allowance from these pages onto tracing paper. Transfer to folded fabric for end pieces. Cut out. Clip and turn edges under ½", and machine-stitch close to edge. Hand-stitch circles to each end.

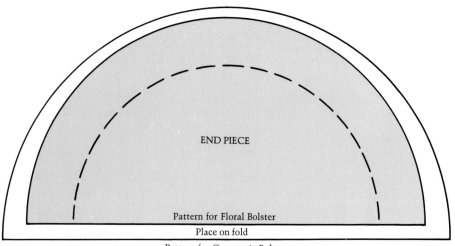

END PIECE

Pattern for Floral Bolster

Place on fold

Pattern for Geometric Bolster

Four-sided stitch ▭▭▭   Satin stitch ≣║║≣

Blue lines represent the individual threads of woven fabric. Black lines indicate embroidered stitches. Squares represent four-sided stitch; close-grouped parallel lines indicate satin stitch. Each four-sided stitch is three threads square, and each satin stitch extends over four threads. Count threads carefully.

FLORAL BOLSTER

Four-sided stitch and satin stitch decorate this bolster. The finished product measures 16″ long and 12″ around. The seam allowance is 1½″.

Shop for these items

Even weave linen or other fabric, about 18 threads per inch, 1 piece 15 x 19″, pink or desired color.

Fabric of similar or firmer weave for interlining and end pieces (broadcloth is good), 1 piece 15 x 25″ (if you are using a prefabricated bolster, interlining is optional, and you will need only 1 6 x 9″ piece for the ends).

26″ of pre-ruffled eyelet trim, 2½″ wide.

Six-strand embroidery floss, 2 skeins white or desired color.

Mercerized cotton, size 8, 2 skeins white or desired color.

Cotton sewing thread to match fabric.

Polyester fiberfill or prefabricated bolster, 16″ long and 12″ around.

Tracing paper.

1 embroidery needle.

Dressmaker's carbon paper.

Cutting and embroidering

Measurements include a very deep seam allowance of 1½″. This allows for fraying of the edges during embroidery, and makes basting unnecessary.

Pulled-thread embroidery—give each stitch a tug. Don't use an embroidery hoop.

Use a double strand of size 8 mercerized cotton for the four-sided stitch and a double strand of embroidery floss for the satin stitch. Embroider stitches consistently in one direction. Satin stitch should be worked either from left to right, or from right to left. Four-sided stitch can be embroidered either horizontally or vertically. Work in the manner most comfortable to you. Give each stitch, particularly the four-sided stitch, a tug to group and separate the threads of fabric and create an openwork effect.

Cut 2 pieces of fabric 15 x 19″, one of the linen and one of the interlining material. You will need a strip 6 x 9″ left over for the end pieces.

Mark center of fabric. To make pattern symmetrical, begin embroidery halfway along one side edge and work towards lower edge, keeping embroidery about ½″ inside seam allowance (2″ from raw edges). Turn work and complete design in the opposite direction to mirror the first half. Repeat the design along the opposite side edge. Establish the framework of four-sided stitches first, and then fill in the satin stitch motifs.

Joining the ruffle

Pin the eyelet ruffle to the right side of the embroidered linen along the 2 side edges, right side down, with the ruffled edge facing in and the other edge of the ruffle extending slightly past the seam allowance. Machine-baste along seam allowance. Turn seam allowance under and press so that ruffle extends outward from fabric edge. Turn the unruffled edges of the linen, and all four edges of the interlining, under 1½″ and press. Place linen and interlining together with right sides out, and machine-stitch close to edge of fabric. (If you have no interlining, follow this step without it.) Remove basting threads.

Hand-stitch the unruffled edges together to form a cylinder and stuff. Fold ends of ruffle around each other and hand-stitch.

Making and joining the end pieces

Trace the semicircle and its seam allowance from these pages onto tracing paper. Transfer to folded fabric for end pieces. Cut out. Clip and turn edges under ½″. Machine-stitch close to edge. Hand-stitch circles to either end.

Four-sided stitch ⊏⊐⊐⊐   Satin stitch ≣⦀⦀≣

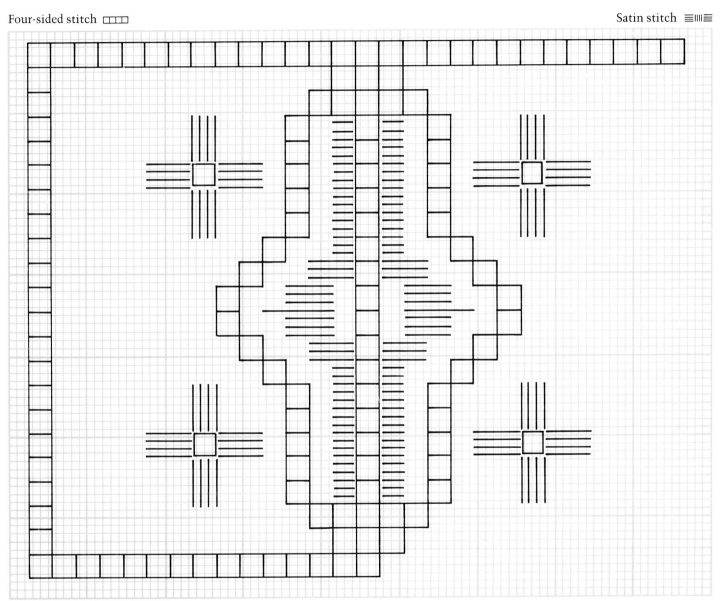

Blue lines represent the individual threads of woven fabric. Black lines indicate embroidered stitches. Squares represent four-sided stitch; close-grouped parallel lines indicate satin stitch. Each four-sided stitch is three threads square, and satin stitches extend over either three or six threads. Count threads carefully.

CROSS STITCH PILLOW

Cross stitch is used to embroider the flowers; satin stitch and four-sided stitch decorate the borders of this pillow. Finished pillow measures 10 x 10" square, excluding the ruffle. The seam allowance is 1½".

Shop for these items

Even weave linen or other fabric, about 24 threads per inch, 1 piece 13 x 13", white or desired color.

Fabric of similar or firmer weave for interlining and backing, 1 piece 26 x 13" (if you use a prefabricated pillow insert for stuffing, interlining is optional, and you will need only 1 piece 13 x 13" for backing).

44" pre-ruffled eyelet trim, 2½" wide.

Six-strand embroidery floss, 1 skein each light pink, medium pink, olive green, medium light green, and white, or desired colors; 2 shades of one color for flower tops, 3 shades of another for stems and leaves, and 1 skein of a third color for the borders.

Cotton sewing thread to match fabric.

1 embroidery needle.

Polyester fiberfill or prefabricated pillow insert, 10 x 10" square.

Cutting and embroidering

A very deep seam allowance of 1½" is included in the measurements. This allows for fraying during embroidery, and makes basting unnecessary.

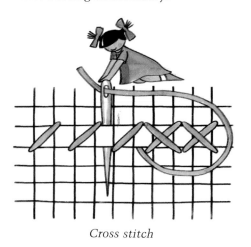

Cross stitch

Embroider your stitches consistently in one direction—satin stitch, back stitch, and cross stitch either from right to left, or left to right. Take care that in cross stitch your bottom stitches all slant one way, and your top stitches slant the opposite way. Four-sided stitch can be worked either horizontally or vertically. Work in the manner most comfortable to you. Use four strands of embroidery floss for the pulled-thread stitches, and three strands for the cross stitch and back stitch.

Cut 3 pieces of fabric 13 x 13"; one piece of linen for embroidering, one interlining, and one backing.

Following the embroidery chart, work from the borders toward the center. First work the double row of adjacent four-sided stitches all around, then the double row of satin stitches all around, then the

short diagonal of 3 four-sided stitches extending from each corner, and one four-sided stitch above and between each group of satin stitches. Embroider the squares of four-sided and satin stitches within each corner of the finished border. Center 4 clusters of flowers in cross stitch and back stitch between the little squares and extending past them.

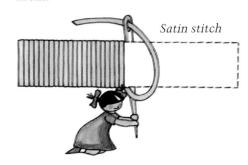

Satin stitch

Putting the pillow together

Machine-baste interlining to wrong side of linen, ½" from edge (if you don't have an interlining, proceed without it). Pin the eyelet ruffle to the right side of embroidery, right side down, with ruffled edge facing in, and other edge extending slightly past the seam allowance. Overlap ends of ruffle ½" and trim excess. Turn ends under ¼" and fold them around each other. Machine-stitch ruffle to fabric directly on seam allowance.

Position backing fabric over embroidered fabric, right sides together. Pin and sew seam directly over previous stitching line, leaving an opening for turning and stuffing (if you are using fiberfill, 2" or 3" is sufficient; if you are using a premade pillow, a larger opening is necessary). Clip and trim seams. Turn pillow right side out and stuff. Hand-stitch opening closed, and sew ends of ruffle together.

Four-sided stitch ⊐⊓⊐   Satin stitch ≡|||≡

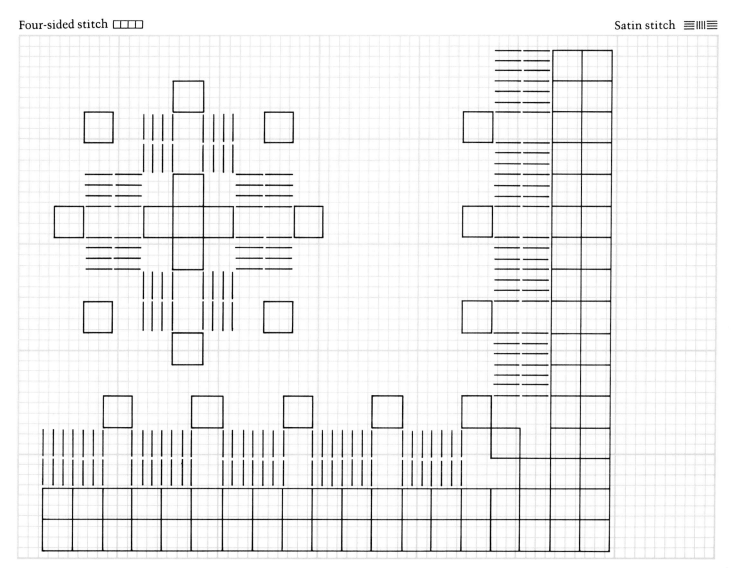

Shown here is the pattern of pulled-thread embroidery, which forms the border of the pillow, and the square motif, which is repeated in each corner of the border. Blue lines represent individual threads of woven fabric. Black lines indicate embroidered stitches. Each square is a four-sided stitch, and each lone vertical is a satin stitch. Give each stitch a tug as you make it to group same thread of the fabric together and separate others. This creates the openwork pattern of holes that is characteristic of pulled-thread work.

Light pink cross stitch   o o o
Medium pink cross stitch o • o
Olive green cross stitch   ◄ ◄

Medium light green **cross stitch** ── ──
Olive green back stitch   - - -

Satin stitch
Four-sided stitch

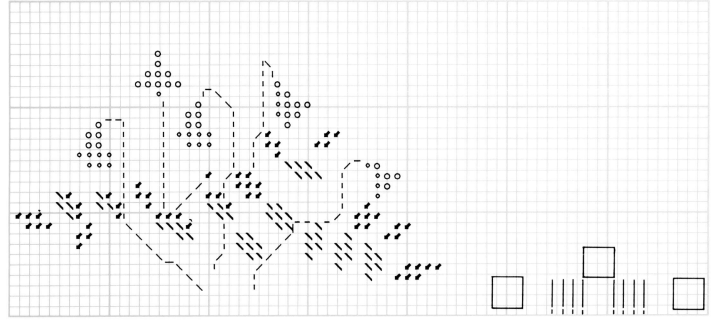

After establishing the border and corner motifs, embroider the flowers. A portion of one corner motif is reproduced in this chart to show you where to place the flow- ers. The broken lines that form the flower stems are worked in back stitch. All other symbols represent cross stitch, a different symbol for each color. Unlike pulled- *thread work, these stitches are intended to cover the surface of the fabric, and should be worked with a fairly slack tension.*

HEART-SHAPED PILLOW

Our heart-shaped pillow is embroidered with four-sided stitch and satin stitch. The finished pillow measures 7" across at the widest point, and 6" down the center of the heart excluding the ruffle. Pattern measurements include 1½" seam allowance.

Shop for these items

Even weave linen or other fabric, about 18 threads per inch, 1 piece 11 x 11", off-white or desired color.
Fabric similar or firmer weave for backing and interlining, 1 piece 11 x 22" (if you are using a prefabricated pillow insert, interlining is optional, and you will need only 1 piece 12 x 12" for backing).
28" of pre-ruffled eyelet trim, 2½" wide.
Six-strand embroidery floss, 2 skeins green or desired color.

1 square = 1"

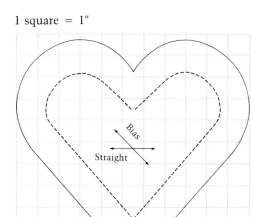

Four-sided stitch ⊏⊐⊐⊐   Satin stitch ≡⦀⦀≡

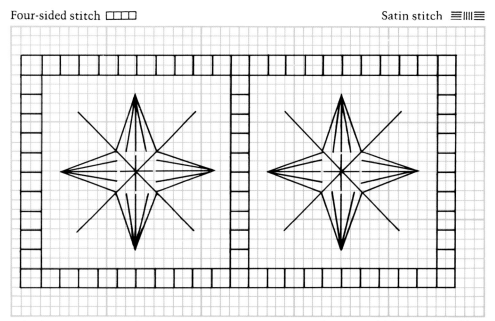

Blue lines represent individual threads of woven fabric. Black lines indicate embroidered stitches. Count threads carefully. Each four-sided stitch is two threads

square. Each square of fabric enclosed by four-sided stitch is 20 threads square. The points of the 4 big flower petals extend to within 2 threads of the edges of the square.

Cotton sewing thread to match fabric.
Polyester fiberfill or prefabricated
   pillow insert of the correct
   dimensions.
1 embroidery needle.
Dressmaker's carbon paper.
Tracing paper.
Water-soluble marking pen.

Marking the fabric

Enlarge the heart pattern from these pages to full-size on tracing paper. If you want the embroidered design to run straight up and down on the pillow, trace the grain arrow that runs straight across the heart. If you want the design to run diagonally, trace the diagonal arrow (we embroidered ours diagonally).

Placing arrow on straight grain of fabric, trace heart and seam allowance onto the linen only. Do not cut out. Go over the outline of the heart and the seam allowance with water-soluble pen.

Embroidering the design

Use two strands of embroidery floss throughout. Embroider your stitches consistently in one direction—satin stitch either from right to left, or left to right; four-sided stitch either horizontally or vertically. Work in the manner most comfortable to you. Extend all the embroidery slightly past the seam allowance.

Embroider first the grid of four-sided stitches. The grid divides the fabric into 20-thread squares. Next, embroider a satin-stitch flower in the center of each square.

Putting the pillow together

Pin three layers of fabric together—the embroidered linen, the interlining, and the backing, with the linen on top, em-

Pulled-thread embroidery—give each stitch a tug. Don't use an embroidery hoop.

broidered side up. Cut out the heart through all three layers. Machine-baste interlining to wrong side of linen, ½" from edge (if you don't have an interlining, proceed without it). Pin the eyelet ruffle to right side of embroidery, with ruffled edge facing in, and other edge of the ruffle extending slightly past the seam allowance. Overlap ends of ruffle ½" and trim excess. Turn ends under ¼" and fold them around each other. Machine-stitch ruffle to fabric directly on seam allowance.

Position backing fabric over embroidered fabric, right sides together. Pin and sew seam directly over previous stitching line, leaving an opening for turning and stuffing (if you are using fiberfill, 2" or 3" is sufficient; if you are using a prefabricated pillow, a larger opening is necessary). Clip and trim seams. Turn pillow right side out and stuff. Hand-stitch opening closed, and sew ends of ruffle together.

Quilted Bunting
and Carriage Blanket

Quilted Bunting and Carriage Blanket

nce you leave the fabric store, with your choice of pre-quilted fabric, you have the worst behind you. Your choice of fabric is an expression of your personal taste, and when you tuck a baby into a handmade bunting it's the next best thing to a loving hug.

The blanket is a mere square of fabric edged with lace. The bunting is made in a T-Shape. It has an elasticized waist to gently encircle the infant, and it closes with a zipper. If you prefer a different closure, you can easily replace the zipper with a strip of velcro or with ribbon ties.

A seam allowance of ½" is included in the pattern and instructions. The finished bunting measures 25" long, 32" around, and 28½" from sleeve edge to sleeve edge. The finished blanket measures 42½" square, excluding the ruffle. Zig-zag or overcast all exposed seams.

Shop for these items
Quilted fabric, 45" wide.
Sewing thread to match fabric.
Dressmaker's carbon paper.
Tissue or tracing paper.
For bunting, 1⅔ yds. fabric.
   1 zipper, 22" long.
   1 package extra wide bias tape, desired color.
   21" of ¼" elastic.
For blanket, 45" fabric.
   Pre-ruffled eyelet lace trim, 1" wide, 5 yds.
   4 yds. of fold-over bias tape, desired color.

BUNTING

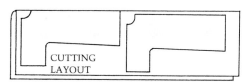

CUTTING LAYOUT

Cutting and marking the fabric
Enlarge and trace pattern pieces onto tissue paper. Transfer all markings. Cut out paper pattern and pin to fabric, following the cutting layout. Transfer all makings from pattern to fabric with dressmaker's carbon. Cut out fabric.

Putting the pieces together

1. Sew center front seam from mark on pattern to bottom edge of center front.

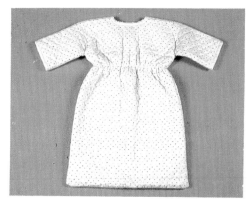

2. Stitch zipper into center front opening.

3. Sew shoulder and sleeve seams at ½".

4. Enclose sleeve ends in bias tape. Edgestitch.

5. Stitch side seams at ½". Stitch lower edge seam at ½". Trim corners diagonally.

6. Enclose neck edge with bias tape. Fold in ends of bias tape at center front to finish.

7. Apply bias tape to form casing on inside 2½″ below underarm all around. Insert 21″ pieces of elastic. Anchor elastic close to center front of garment.

BLANKET

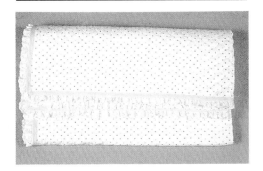

Cutting, edging, and finishing

Cut quilted fabric to a 42½ x 42½″ square. Place wrong sides of lace and fabric together. Sew lace to edge with ¼″ seam allowance, mitering lace at corners. Press seam allowance away from lace edge.

Cover seam allowance with finished ½″ bias. Slip-stitch or edgestitch along both edges, thereby enclosing seam allowance. Miter bias at corners.

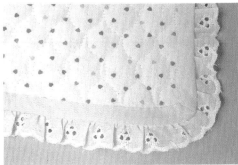

Miter the ruffle at each corner of the blanket by allowing a little extra fullness as you join it. Miter the bias by tucking it into a diagonal at each corner. The bias can be attached by hand, with slip-stitching or by machine, with edge stitching.

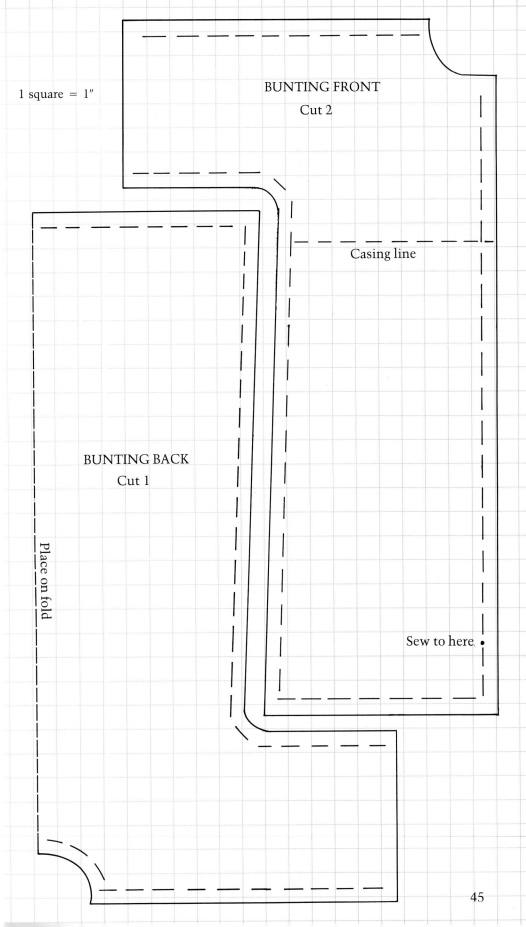

1 square = 1″

BUNTING FRONT
Cut 2

Casing line

BUNTING BACK
Cut 1

Place on fold

Sew to here

Rabbit Quilt

Frrom all directions, rabbits bound into the lives of children. Smart-alecky cartoon rabbits. Easter bunnies with baskets of eggs. Rabbits pulled out of hats. Overconfident, nap-taking hares. Short-lived chocolate bunnies. Pale, nervous, respectably dressed, unpunctual rabbits, leading gleeful, curious children down ponderous pathways to fantastic regions. Rabbits seem to be tailor-made for caricature and fantasy, with their long ears and front teeth, quivering pink noses, pouffy tails, vegetarian diets, and eccentric means of locomotion. Look where one led Alice.

We have therefore designed a rabbit quilt. The front is pieced together in five panels. A large quilted rabbit occupies the central panel, with a collection of carrots quilted into the top, bottom, and side panels.

We used white fabric, white quilting thread, and white quilt binding, for a sort of rabbit-eating-a-carrot-in-a-snowstorm effect. We then framed the center panel with bias tape in a contrasting color and tacked bows at the frames corners.

Our directions suggest tracing the design onto the fabric with a water-soluble pen, available in needlework stores. Test the ink on a fabric scrap before using it on the quilt. The lines should be easily removable with a wet cloth.

Rabbit quilt, when finished, measures 42 x 54". Seam allowances are ½".

Shop for these items

Cotton broadcloth, 45" wide, 3⅛ yds. white or desired color.
2 packages (6 yds.) of double fold quilt binding, white or desired color.
2 packages (8 yds.) of double fold bias tape, contrasting color (we used blue).
Cotton sewing thread to match fabric.
Extra-strong quilting thread, desired color (we used ecru).
Quilt batting, 1 bag, washable.
Quilting needles, #8.
1 Quilting hoop.
Water-soluble pen.
Tissue or tracing paper.

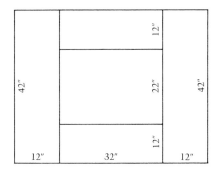

Cutting and making the fabric

Cut five panels for the front; top and bottom panels, 12 x 42", side panels, 12 x 32", and center panel, 22 x 32". Cut a single 42 x 54" piece for the back.

Enlarge and trace the design onto tissue paper. To transfer the design to the fabric, position and pin down the tracing on the cloth. With a blunt tapestry needle or small size knitting needle, puncture holes along the lines of the design. Go through the holes with water soluble pen. Remove the tracing, and connect the dots on the fabric with the same pen. Transfer the rabbit to the center panel, and arrange carrots on the top, bottom, and side panels. (If you prefer, you can trace down the designs with dress maker's carbon, and go over the lines with the pen afterward).

Piecing and quilting

Piece together the front panels with ½" seam allowance. Side panels fit between top and bottom panels. Press the seam allowances together (do not press seams open in quilting).

1 square = 1"

Before you start to quilt, baste together the three layers—the pieced front panel, the quilt batting, and back panel, with right sides of fabric facing out.

Insert quilt into quilting hoop. Work even running stitches with the quilting thread through all three layers, along the lines of the design.

Finishing the quilt

Remove all pen lines with water and a clean cloth. Lay the bias tape in the front of the quilt, centering it on the seamline around the center panel. Tack down seamline around the center panel. Tack down with small slip-stitches. Cut 4 12" lengths of bias, fold each one in half. Tack down at this halfway point to each corner of the bias square now on the quilt. Tie in bows.

Slip-stitch the quilt binding around the outer edges of the quilt, mitering at corners. Remove pen lines with a wet cloth.

This is the front of the finished quilt. With a quilting needle and extra strong quilting thread, the lines of the design are worked in small, even running stitches through three layers—the front and back fabrics and the quilt batting. Bias tape is tacked down around the center panel, and a bow is placed at each corner.

Farmyard Quilt with Appliquéd Animals

Nurseries should shelter life and stimulate curiosity. This is a nursery quilt that introduces the young ones to the mystery of other living things. At bedtime, it may also inspire the inventiveness of a parent to spin a homemade yarn or remember a rhyme from childhood.

The front is made up of a large central rectangle, with a farmhouse and 16 surrounding squares, each with a different animal appliquéd and embroidered on it. The quilting stitches bring the outlines of the house and animals through to the back panel of the quilt, which is made up of a single piece of light-colored fabric (we used blue).

As the appliqué and embroidery are done before piecing the front together, this quilt is a project that a number of different people can collaborate on. It is an heirloom which can later be hung as a decorative wall piece. One day it could bridge the gap between yesterday and today.

Farmyard quilt, when finished, measures 42 x 62". The seam allowances on the front panel are 1" and ¼" on the appliqué. The stitches used are running stitch, stem stitch, and French knots.

Shop for these items
Cotton broadcloth, 45" wide
  2 yds. white
  3 yds. blue
  ⅓ yd. each of light purple, rust, pink, orange, light salmon, red, dark brown, and gray, or desired colors.
Cotton sewing thread to match fabric.
Extra strong quilting thread (we used blue to match the blue fabric).
Six-strand embroidery floss, 1 skein each light salmon, medium salmon, light apricot, yellow, medium gray, dark gray, red, purple, brown, or desired colors to embroider house and animal features.

Quilting needles, #8 or 9.
1 bag of quilt batting, washable, and of uniform thickness.
1 quilting hoop.
Dressmaker's carbon paper.
Tissue or tracing paper.
Water-soluble tracing pen.

Cutting and marking the fabric
Cut the panels for the front: 1 center panel, while 22 x 42", 12 blue 12 x 12" squares and 4 white 12 x 12" squares. Cut one blue piece for the back, 44 x 64".

Enlarge and trace the designs onto tissue paper. Using dressmaker's carbon, transfer the house to the center front panel, and the animals to different colored, fabrics. Go over the lines of the house with water-soluble pen.

Adding ¼" all around for seam allowance, cut out animal shapes.

Applying and decorating the animals
Notch animal seam allowances every ⅜" along curved edges. Turn edges under ¼" and baste an animal into place on each 12 x 12 square. With matching sewing thread and tiny slip-stitches, securely sew each animal to its panel. Remove basting stiches.

Running stitch

Embroider features and details on the different animals with stem stitch and French knots, using three strands of embroidery floss. The animals themselves are joined to the front panel with tiny, neat slip-stitches of matching sewing thread.

With a soft pencil, mark and outline details on the animals, such as wings, tails, beaks and bills, eyes and ears, noses and feet. Using different colors of embroidery floss, triple-strand, embroider these details with stem stitch and French knots.

Quilting and embroidering

Piece front panels together using 1 seam allowance. Trim allowances ½" and press down together (do not press seams open in quilting).

Before you start to quilt, baste together the three layers—the pieced front panel, the quilt batting, and the back panel, with right sides of fabric facing out. The back panel edges should extend past the front by 1" all around.

Insert quilt into quilting hoop. With quilting thread, using the running stich, quilt all around each animal, placing the sitches just outside the edges of the appliqué (this is called "quilting in the valley"), and work along the lines of the house on the center panel. Work through all thicknesses.

Edging the quilt

Turn the edges of the back panel under ¼", then fold again at ¾", enclosing the batting and front panel edges. Secure with neat slip-stitches. Remove basting threads.

1 square = 1"

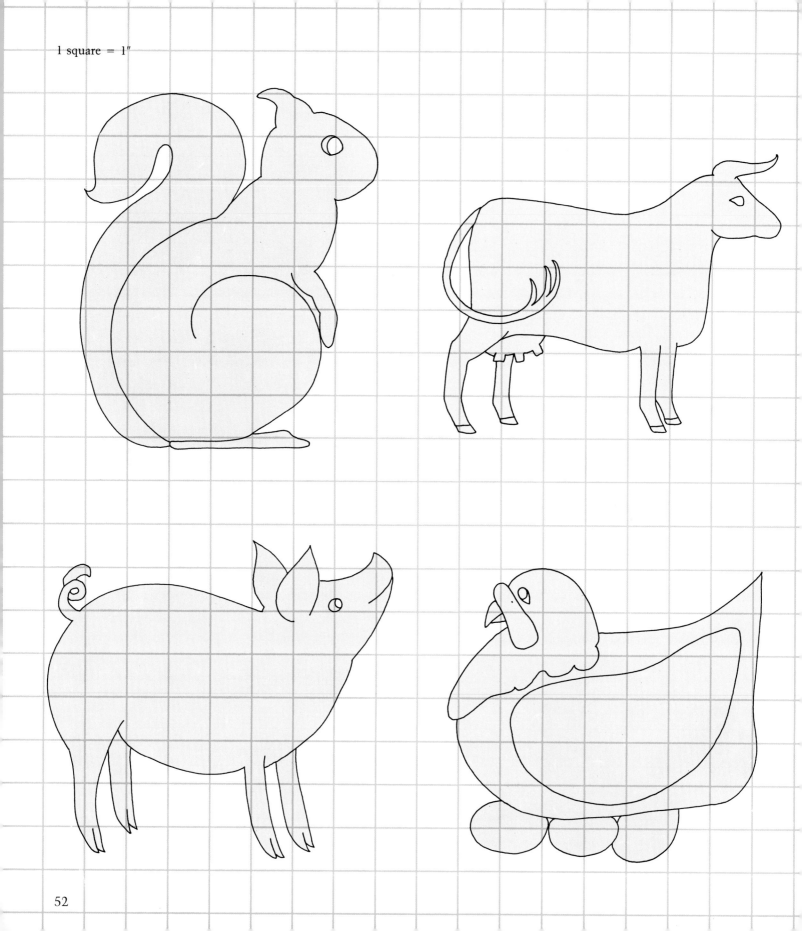

52

1 square = 1″

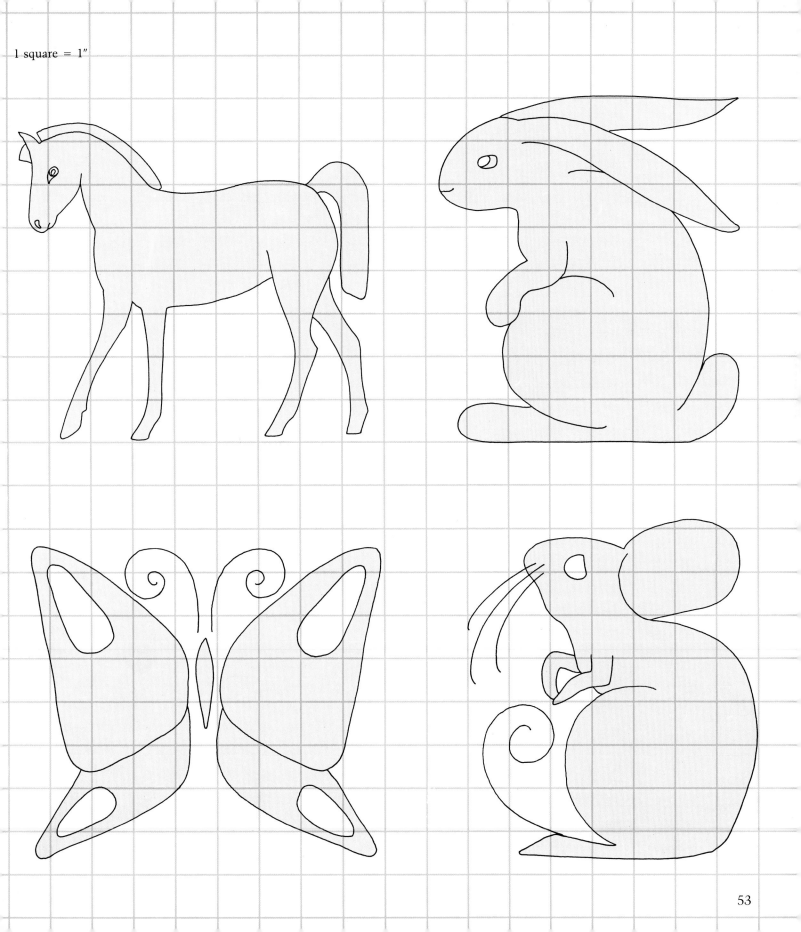

1 square = 1″

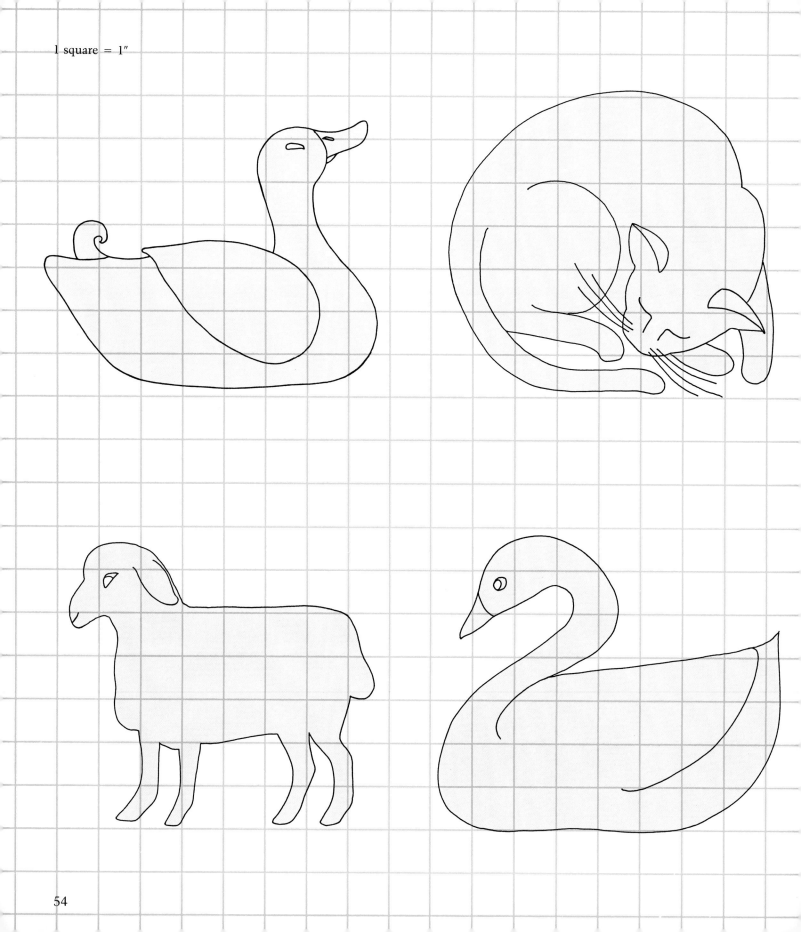

1 square = 2″

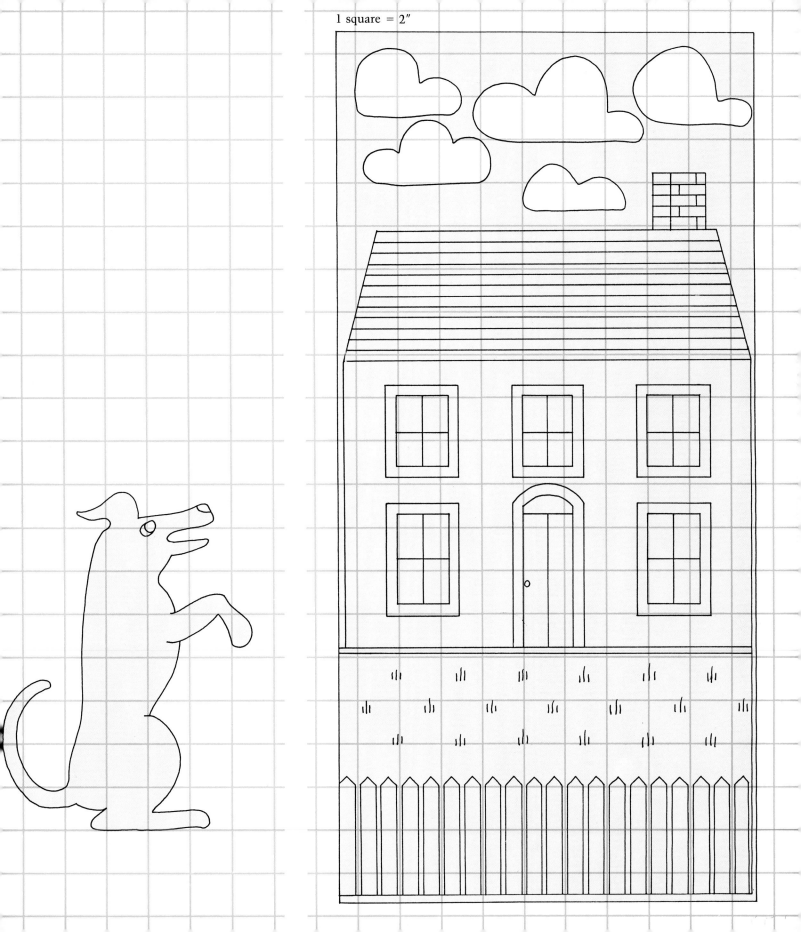

3.

*Party Clothes,
sewn and tailored
to pass down*

Lace-trimmed Batiste Dress and Slip

A little girl can't help looking picturesque in this light summer dress. Sewn in fine cotton batiste and laces, with a matching slip, it is Victorian charm in a contemporory shape. The skirt is full and gathered. The texture of the lace edgings and inserts, and of the embroidered batiste edging around the hem provide all the detail the dress needs.

You will find both the dress and slip surprisingly easy to make. No hand stitching is necessary, except to attach the single button at the back neck closure. All hems and neck openings are lace-edged. The steps that look most difficult, the criss-crossed and vertical lace insertions on the dress front, only require that you stitch straight and cut straight.

Make it for a two-to three-year-old in whitest whites, and pose her in it with a red ribbon and a basket of strawberries to make a picture she can later show her children.

Garment instructions and measurements are for size 2, and include ¼" seam allowance. Pink, zig-zag, or overcast to finish exposed seams (not lace joinings).

Shop for these items

Fabric: 36" wide cotton batiste, white.
Lace insertion: ½" wide, white.
Lace edging: ⅜" wide, white.
Embroidered batiste edging: 2½" wide, white.
Cotton sewing thread, white.
For slip, 1 yd. fabric. 1½ yds. lace edging.
For dress, 1 yds. fabric.
  2 yds. lace edging.
  7 yds. insertion lace.

CUTTING LAYOUT

1½ yds. batiste edging.
1 button, ¼" wide mother-of-pearl.

Cutting and marking the fabric

Enlarge and trace pattern pieces onto tissue paper. Transfer all markings. Cut out paper pattern pieces and pin to fabric, following the cutting layout. Transfer all markings with dressmaker's carbon and cut out.

Before you start

Lace edging technique
There are two methods of applying lace edgings to the slip and dress. Use the one you prefer. We used method 2 in our sample.
Method 1: Place edging along raw fabric edge, overlapping fabric ¼" on right side (edge of lace is on seam allowance). Zig-zag along edge of lace. Carefully trim away excess fabric on wrong side.
Method 2: Turn raw edge of fabric under ⅛" twice. Overlap lace ⅛" over fabric edge on right side of garment. Topstitch through lace and folded fabric.

Lace insertion technique
There are two methods of applying the lace insertions to the dress front. Use the

one you prefer. We used method 2 in our sample.

Method 1: Center insertion lace on lace placement line, right side of fabric. Zigzag along outermost edges of lace. Carefully slit the fabric behind the lace and trim away as close as possible to stitching.

Method 2: Center insertion lace on lace placement line, right side of fabric. Stitch lace along its outermost edges. Carefully slit the fabric behind the lace, cutting halfway between stitching lines. Fold back the raw edges of fabric and press. Stitch again from right side, as close to first stitching line as possible. Trim raw edges of fabric close to second stitching.

DRESS

1. Apply a strip of ½″ insertion lace to lower edge of back yoke pieces.

Gather upper edges of back dress at ¼″. Adjust gather to fit lace strip just applied to back yoke, and apply free edge of lace to gathered edge.

Make one left and one right back. Stitch center back seam at ¼″ up to dot. Press seam open. Apply a double row of ½″ insertion lace to lower back edge, overlapping the second strip slightly over the first and topstitching. Stitch batiste edging to second row lace at scant ¼″, right sides of edging and lace together. Press seam allowance towards hem. Edgestitch on right side of batiste edging.

2. Open out front. Apply ½″ lace insertions to front, following placement lines and numbered sequence. First insert the center diagonals, then the inner vertical lines, then the outer verticals.

3. Apply a strip of ½″ insertion lace to bottom edge of front yoke. Gather top edge of front dress to fit lace strip just applied to yoke. Apply free edge of lace to gathered edge of front.

Apply a double row of insertion lace to lower edge of front. Join batiste edging to second row of lace in same manner as back.

4. Join shoulders with ¼″ seam. Press open.

5. Apply ½″ insertion lace to outer edges of sleeves, allowing lace to form ½″ loops at the 2 points. Join a row of ⅜″ lace edging around edge of insertion lace.

Gather sleeve cap between notches at ¼″. Sew in sleeves at ¼″, matching shoulder seams to sleeve center and adjusting gathers evenly between notches.

6. Join side seams of dress at ¼″.

7. Apply ⅜″ lace edging to neck opening.

8. Fold under edges of center back opening, beginning with ⅛″ fold at top and tapering to nothing where opening meets seam; stitch. Fold and stitch again.

9. If possible, try the dress on the child for fit. Mark placement of button and buttonhole at upper edge of center back opening. Work buttonhole and sew on button.

1 square = 1″   ¼″ seam allowance throughout

Shown here are the finished lower edge of the dress, and two of the vertical lace insertions on the front (step 2). Insertions are made by stitching the lace down along marked lines and cutting away the fabric behind the lace. On the lower edge of the dress, a delicate embroidered batiste edging is added to a double row of insertion lace (steps 1 and 3).

The dress sleeve is edged first with a strip of ½″ insertion lace and then with a strip of ⅜″ lace edging. While joining the first strip, pause in the stitching to make a small loop at each of the 2 points on the fabric edge (Step 5). Insertion lace is straight on both edges; edgings are straight on the joining edge and frilly or scalloped on the outer edge.

SLIP FRONT
Cut 1

Place on fold

SLIP

1. Sew shoulder seams at ¼″.

2. Apply lace edging around neck edge. Overlap ends of lace and finish.

3. Apply lace to armhole edges.

4. Sew side seams at ¼″, catching lace ends in seam.

5. Edge hem of slip with ½″ insertion lace. Overlap ends of lace and finish.

Shoulder

Neck edge

FRONT YOKE
Cut 1 on fold

Place on fold

Neck edge   Shoulder

Center Back

BACK YOKE
Cut 2

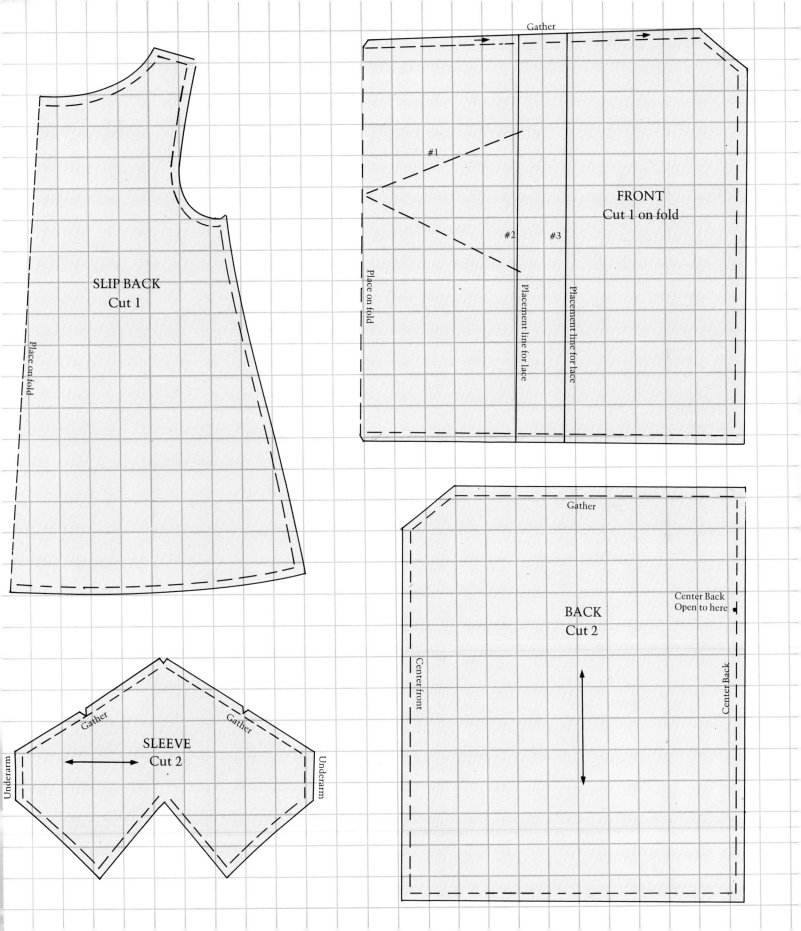

SLIP BACK
Cut 1

Place on fold

FRONT
Cut 1 on fold

Gather

#1

#2 #3

Place on fold

Placement line for lace

Placement line for lace

BACK
Cut 2

Gather

Center Back
Open to here

Center front

Center Back

SLEEVE
Cut 2

Gather Gather

Underarm Underarm

Please come to
my First
Birthday Party

Party Dress with English Smocking

The mood of this quietly beautiful dress is created by making a simple raglan shape with a small-print fabric and augmenting it with fine hand-embroidery and delicate hand-finishing. All you need are a pair of loving hands, a few materials, and a determination not to stint on a single detail—neither pleating nor smocking nor thread-loop closure.

Below the hand-embroidered, smocked and pleated yoke, the dress billows out comfortably, to accomodate the furies, festivities, and fatigue of a 2-year old. It is perfect spring or Easter attire.

The yoke is worked in cable, wave, and trellis stitches with a triple strand of embroidery floss. The short puffed sleeves are elasticized at the hem. The dress fastens in back with two small buttons and hand-worked thread loops.

We recommend making this dress of a cotton or cotton-blend fabric, for crispness and breathability.

The instructions are for size 2. Changes for size 4 are given in parentheses.

Shop for these items
1⅝ yds of 45" wide cotton or cotton-blend fabric.
Sewing thread to match fabric.
½ yd of ¼" elastic.
Two ⅜" buttons (we used mother-of-pearl buttons).
1 skein of cotton embroidery floss.
5 18 x 24" sheets tissue paper or other paper (to make paper pattern).
Dressmaker's carbon paper (for pattern).
Dot transfer pattern (for pleating).
Button or carpet thread (for pleating).

Cutting and marking the fabric
Refer to the cutting layout to mark and cut the proper rectangles out of paper for the size you are making. Use the paper pattern pieces and follow the cutting layout to cut the following rectangles from the fabric on the correct grain. *Note:* ½" seam allowances are included in the measurements. Always double-check before you cut!
2 backs—16 (16¼)" wide by 22 x ¼ (23¼)" long.

1 front, cut on the fold—13½ (13¾)" wide [27 (27½)" unfolded] by 21½ (22¼)" long.
2 sleeves—15¾ (16)" wide by 9¼ (9½)" long.
1 neckband, cut on the bias—1¾ (1¾)" wide by 12 (12½)" long.

Trace the actual-size raglan cutting lines for the size you are making onto tissue paper (size 2 is in red, size 4 in blue). Matching side and top edges, pin the tissue to the fabric rectangles, positioning raglan lines as shown in the cutting layout. Cut along the raglan lines. Transfer single notch to dress front and sleeve front, double notches to dress back and sleeve back.

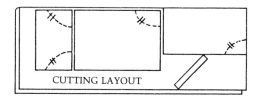

CUTTING LAYOUT

Putting the pieces together
1. With right sides of fabric together, matching notches, sew sleeves to front and back along raglan seamlines.

2. Starting ⅝" below raw neck edge, and leaving ½" free at either edge of center back opening, mark neckline area on wrong side of fabric with 10 evenly spaced (⅜" apart) rows of dots. Run a pleating thread along each row of dots. Gather threads to form a pleated yoke, measuring 11½ (12)" across.

3. Following the Smocking Chart, using three strands of embroidery floss, work smocking as follows:
Row 1 and 2: Work a row of cable st across first row of pleating. Rep across 2nd row of pleating.
Row 3, 4, 5: Beg with point at center front of dress, work trellis st from center to right edge. Turn work upside down, return to center front point, and complete design in the opposite direction. Smocking sts are placed on the rows of pleating and halfway between them.
Row 6-10: Beg with point at center front of dress on row 10, work 3 rows of closely spaced wave st from left to right. Turn work upside down, return to center front point, and complete design in the opposite direction. Smocking sts are worked on rows of pleating and ⅓ and ⅔ of the way between them.

4. Steam-press smocking lightly and remove pleating threads. If pleats lose shape between smocking, you may want to touch them up with rows of outline st on the wrong side with embroidery floss to match fabric.

5. To form back placket, shallowly clip edges of center back opening from neck edge to beg of seamline (7" below neck edge). Turn each clipped edge under ¼" twice; slip-stitch in place.

6. With right sides of fabric together, matching raw edges, pin neckband to neck opening, extending ends of neckband ¼" beyond edges of center back placket. Stitch. Press band towards neck. Fold ends of band under ¼". Fold band to inside. Turn under ¼" on raw edge and slip-stitch to neckline.

7. Turn each sleeve edge under ¼", then ³⁄₈" for sleeve casings. Stitch close to edge.

8. With right sides together, sew each side and sleeve seam in a continuous operation from above sleeve casing to lower edge. Press seams open.

9. Cut 2 pieces of elastic 8½ (9)" long (or the circumference of the child's arm, plus 1"). Insert the elastic into the casing, overlap ends 1" and sew together. Stitch opening.

10. Sew 2 buttons to left side of placket, one at neckband and one 2" below. Make 2 loops of thread; each loop emerges from edge of placket opposite a button. Each loop should be just a thread's width longer than necessary to hold the 2 sides of the placket gently together when buttoned. Work blanket st tightly along the full length of the loop.

11. Turn up a bottom hem of 2¼" and baste in place. If possible, try the dress on the child for adjustment. Slip-stitch hem in place.

Wrong-side-out view of dress, showing left side, sleeve, and raglan seams. Note that the seam that closes the sleeve underneath and continues down the side of the dress is sewn in one continuous run from cuff to hem.

Top back of completed dress, wrong side out, showing the yoke, placket opening, and neckband. The yoke pleating and smocking are done after joining the raglan seams. The steps for the neckband, placket, sleeve casings, side and sleeve seams, hem, and buttonloops follow the completion of the yoke.

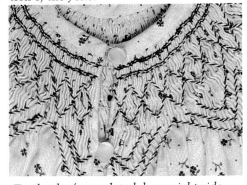

Top back of completed dress, right side out, shows the back button fastening. The thread loops are more elegant than buttonholes and give a cleaner, more precise closure because the edges of the opening butt each other, rather than overlap. See Step 12.

Cable stitch smocking is worked along the top rows of pleating (pleating threads are indicated by broken horizontal lines). The thread is thrown alternately above and below the needle, separating the pleats into pairs, which are re-divided into alternate pairs by the second cable stitch row.

Two zig-zagging rows of trellis stitch smocking meet to form little diamond shapes and decorate the center section of the yoke. The stitches at the zig-zag points come either on the rows of pleating or halfway between them.

Wave stitch smocking decorates the lower section of the dress yoke. It is similar to trellis stitch in technique, but looks like a line of connected "V's" with smaller "V's" inside them. The contrast between thread color and fabric color gives a candy-cane stripe effect to the diagonal lines of stitches.

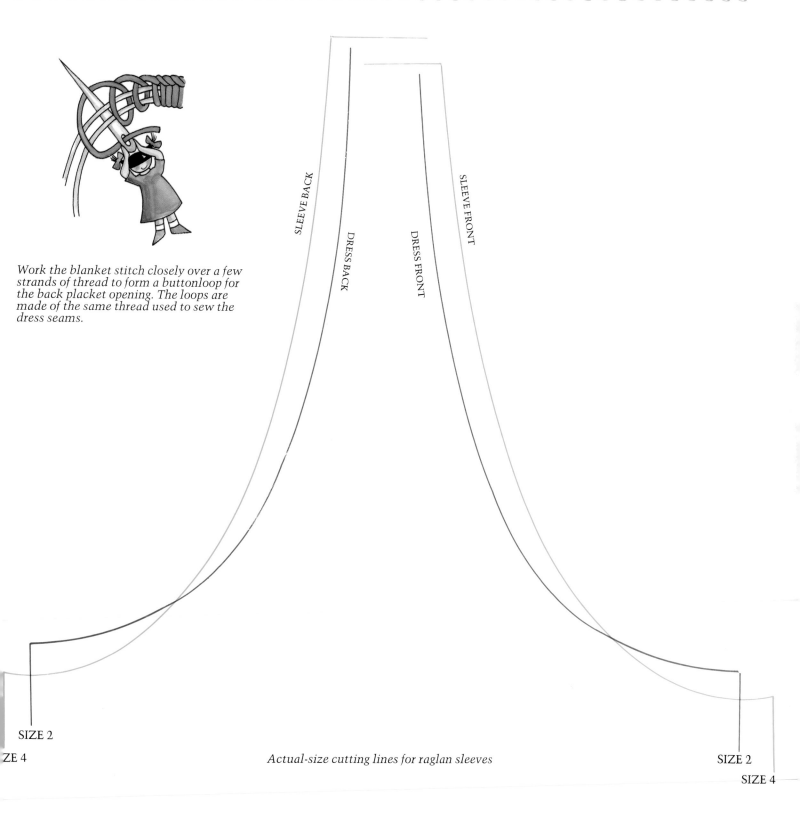

Work the blanket stitch closely over a few strands of thread to form a buttonloop for the back placket opening. The loops are made of the same thread used to sew the dress seams.

SLEEVE BACK

SLEEVE FRONT

DRESS BACK

DRESS FRONT

SIZE 2

ZE 4

SIZE 2

SIZE 4

Actual-size cutting lines for raglan sleeves

Box-Pleated Wool Dress

Make a dress-up dress with pleats that hang in formal symmetry and at the same time provide the fullness that allows for the informal movements of a six-to-18-month-old girl.

It buttons all the way down the back and has short, puffed sleeves and a rounded collar. You cross stitch five butterflies in red and gray on the front yoke. To make the embroidery, a piece of waste canvas is basted to the uncut yoke fabric. Then the embroidery can be worked through both fabric and canvas. When you dampen the canvas it can be removed strand by strand with tweezers.

This is a perfect garment for grown-up little girls to wear on formal occasions. Make it in a soft, lightweight wool or wool-blend fabric that drapes into elegant folds.

Dress pattern and instructions are for size 1. Measurements include ⅝" seam allowance. Pink, zig-zag, or overcast all exposed seams, or use French seams.

Shop for these items

1¼ yds. of 44" wide wool or wool blend fabric (viyella is good), white or desired color.
½ yd. of ¼" wide elastic.
26" of ⅛" satin ribbon.
5 buttons ⅜" wide.
Six-strand embroidery floss, 1 skein each gray and pink, or desired colors.
1 embroidery needle.
Dressmaker's carbon paper.
Tissue or tracing paper (to make pattern).
Waste canvas, 1 piece 4 x 12".
Tweezers.

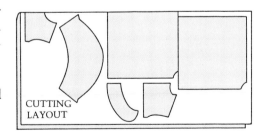

CUTTING LAYOUT

Cutting and marking the fabric

Enlarge pattern pieces shown on grid and trace actual-size pieces from these pages onto tissue paper. Transfer all markings. Cut out paper pattern and pin to folded fabric, following the cutting layout. Transfer all markings from pattern pieces to fabric with dressmaker's carbon. Cut out all pieces except front yoke.

Embroidering the yoke

Baste the waste canvas securely to the wrong side of the front yoke behind the embroidery placement markings. Begin the first half of the design at the marked center of placement line and work towards the left-hand edge until you have completed 2½ butterflies. Return to the center of the fabric, turn the work and the chart around, and embroider the second half of the design in the opposite direction to make 5 finished butterflies. Work each stitch through both the fabric and the canvas. All bottom stitches should slant in one direction, and all top stitches in the other direction. When the embroidery is complete, wet the waste canvas and remove the threads of canvas with tweezers.

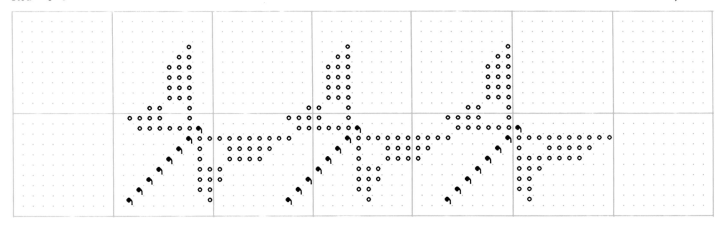

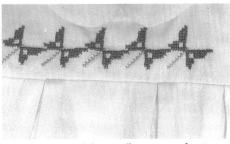

The cross-stitch butterflies are embroidered on the front yoke of the dress before it is cut out. The box-pleats stand out in symmetrical relief on the dress front and backs. They are formed by folding back equal amounts of fabric behind the pleat. See step 1.

An inside view of the collar and neck finishing shows the two collar sections just meeting at the neck front. A hand-cut bias strip covers the raw edges of the seam allowance. See step 8.

1. Cut out the front yoke. Form box pleats on front and backs, folding according to pattern markings. Baste in place. Press.

2. Join front yoke to front dress. Join back yokes to back. Be sure to make one left and one right back.

3. Sew shoulder seams.

4. At center back, turn under ¼" on raw edge. Stitch in place. Turn under 1" to form neck band. Press in place.

5. Run 2 rows of gathering stitches around sleeve cap. Gather sleeve to fit armhole and stitch sleeves to dress.

6. Sew sleeve and dress side seams. Cut 2 pieces of elastic 8" long, or to the child's upper arm measurement, plus ½".

7. Turn up casing on sleeve hem. (To form casing turn up ¼" on raw edge, then turn up again wide enough to allow for stitching and insertion of elastic.) Stitch, leaving opening for elastic. Insert elastic. Overlap ends ½" and stitch ends together. Stitch casing opening closed.

8. Collar is constructed in 2 separate pieces. On each section of collar sew along ⅝" stitching line, leaving neck edge open. Trim down seam allowance to ¼". Clip curves in collar. Trim corners diagonally. Turn right side out and press. Machine-baste neck edge closed. Sew 2 half collars to dress (clipping neck line if necessary), matching center front, shoulder notches and back collar notches. Collars should meet at center front along stitching line. Turn center back fold to front so that collar is sandwiched between fold and yoke. Attach bias strip to neck edge along established stitching line. Bias should be stitched from end to end so that it is enclosed in center back fold. Trim and clip neck seam allowance (now including bias strip, collar and garment) to ¼". Fold down bias and stitch by hand to body of garment.

9. Slip-stitch lining to front yoke by hand, sewing invisibly along all edges.

10. Turn up hem along fold line. Remove pleat basting and attach ⅛" ribbon to raw edge of hem. Blind stitch hem.

11. Following pattern markings, make buttons and buttonholes along center back fold.

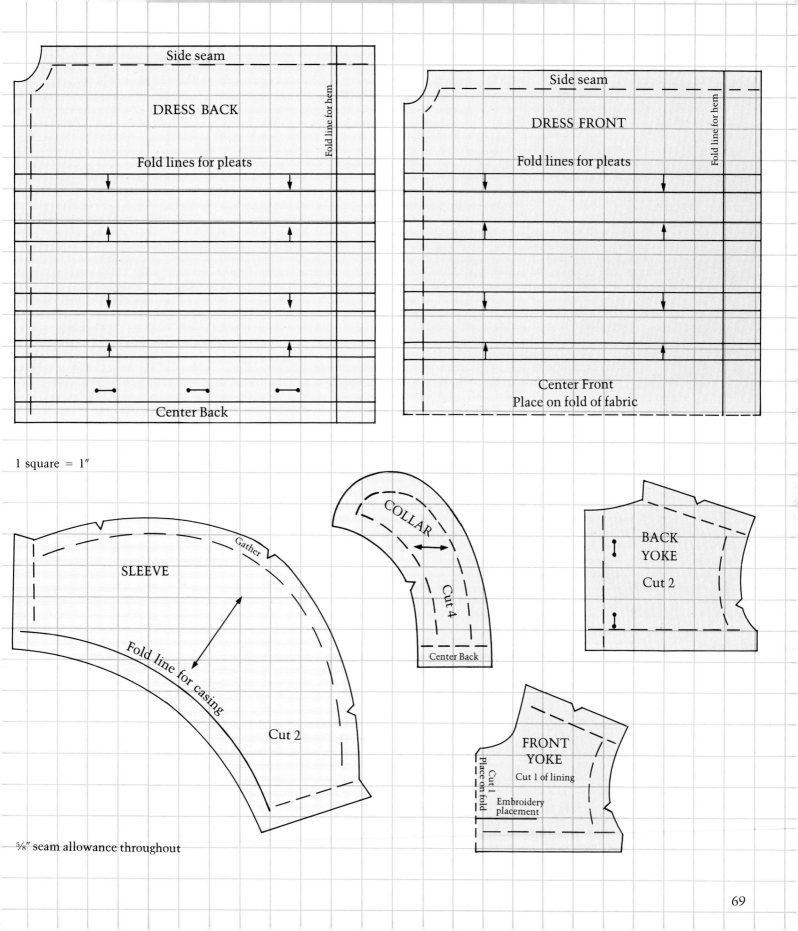

Side seam

DRESS BACK

Fold lines for pleats

Fold line for hem

Center Back

DRESS FRONT

Side seam

Fold lines for pleats

Fold line for hem

Center Front
Place on fold of fabric

1 square = 1″

SLEEVE

Gather

Fold line for casing

Cut 2

COLLAR

Cut 4

Center Back

BACK
YOKE

Cut 2

FRONT
YOKE

Cut 1
Place on fold

Cut 1 of lining

Embroidery
placement

⅝″ seam allowance throughout

Practical Plaids

This self-belted short-sleeved blouse and matching short pants with criss-crossing suspender straps were inspired by an outfit which was favored by the author's son as a toddler.

We used a plaid, navy and white cotton fabric, and matched these colors in the trim. Navy bias tape outlines the details and finishes off the raw edges at the same time. Navy buttons fasten the blouse, belt, and pants straps. The white collar is made in 2 sections which overlap in front.

The diversity of uses for this design makes it an extremely practical gift. It is appropriate for a small child of either sex. The top can be worn with different pants, or as a dress for a little girl, if it is lengthened. The pants will work with different tops and their elasticized waist will stretch or contract to fit various tummy sizes.

Sturdy cotton or cotton-blend fabrics are good choices for an outfit like this one that must withstand everyday wear. You might also want to consider that denim or corduroy would give an interesting rugged look and would hold up best of all.

Pattern and instructions are for size 2. Measurements include ³⁄₈″ seam allowance. Pink, zig-zag, or overcast to finish all exposed seams.

Shop for these items

¾ yard of 45″ wide cotton or cotton blend fabric.
¼ yard of white voile or piqué material for collar.
1 package double-fold bias tape (we used navy).
Sewing thread to match fabric.
1 yard of ¼″ elastic.
7½″ wide buttons (we used navy buttons to match the bias tape).
3 18 x 24″ sheets of tissue or tracing paper (to make pattern).
Dressmaker's carbon paper.

Cutting and marking the fabric

Enlarge pattern pieces shown on grid and trace onto tissue paper. Transfer all markings. Cut out paper pattern and pin to folded fabric, following the cutting layout. Transfer all markings from pattern pieces to fabric with dressmaker's carbon and cut out. Cut 2 pieces of elas-

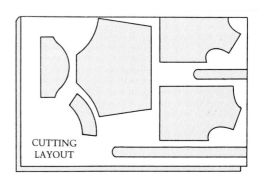

CUTTING LAYOUT

tic 9″ long for pant legs, and one piece 17″ long for waist (includes ½″ overlap).

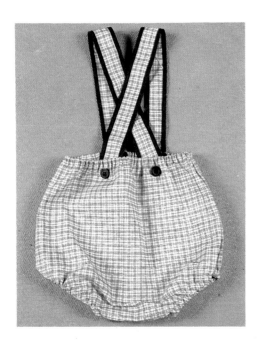

PANTS

1. Sew bias tape around edges of straps, with the raw edges of fabric enclosed in the fold of the tape.

2. Sew side and crotch seams.

3. To make the leg casing, press down scant ¼" around each leg opening. Fold over to form casing for ¼" elastic. Stitch, leaving an opening for elastic. Insert elastic, overlap ends ½", and sew. Stitch opening closed. Elastic should finish at 8".

4. Refer to pattern markings for placement, and sew straps to right side of fabric at pants waist.

5. Make waist casing in same manner as leg casing, finishing elastic at 16".

6. Sew buttons to ends of straps. Make buttonholes on pants where indicated by pattern markings.

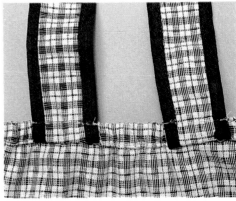

Inside-out view of finished pants, front waist. After the straps are edged with bias tape (step 1), they are sewn to the pants (step 4). The strap ends turn under with the pants edge to form the waist casing (step 5).

BLOUSE

5. Sew each sleeve and side seam in a continuous operation from cuff to hem.

6. Fold center back edges of garment under ½". Fold again and stitch along marked stitching line to form placket. Place 3 buttons and buttonholes according to pattern markings.

7. Sew bias tape around blouse hem with ends of tape folded in to make a finished edge at center back.

8. The collar is constructed in 2 sections. With right sides together, sew seams of each section along 3 sides, leaving neck edge open. Clip points diagonally. Turn right side out and press. Baste neck edges of collars closed. Pin collar sections to right side of blouse, matching neck edges and overlapping the 2 collar pieces at the center front by ¼". Collar should rest ½" from established center backs. Stitch.

1. Sew shoulder seams.

2. While garment is flat, sew in sleeves, matching notch to shoulder seam.

3. Sew bias tape around 2 belt pieces. Refer to pattern markings for placement of belt on front. Stitch ends of belt to front, ¼" from raw edge. Sew buttons to belt and shirt front where marked.

4. Sew bias tape to sleeve hems.

Inside-out view of finished neck edge. The raw edge of the collar/neck edge seam allowance is clipped, trimmed and covered over with bias tape (step 8).

9. Lay garment wrong side up, with collar extended and seam allowance at neck folded toward body. Finish the raw neck edge by joining opened bias tape, wrong side up, sewing the center foldline of the bias tape to the stitching line on the fabric. Trim and clip seam allowances at neck. Fold bias tape toward body of garment and stitch down, with ends of tape folded in to make a finished edge at the center back.

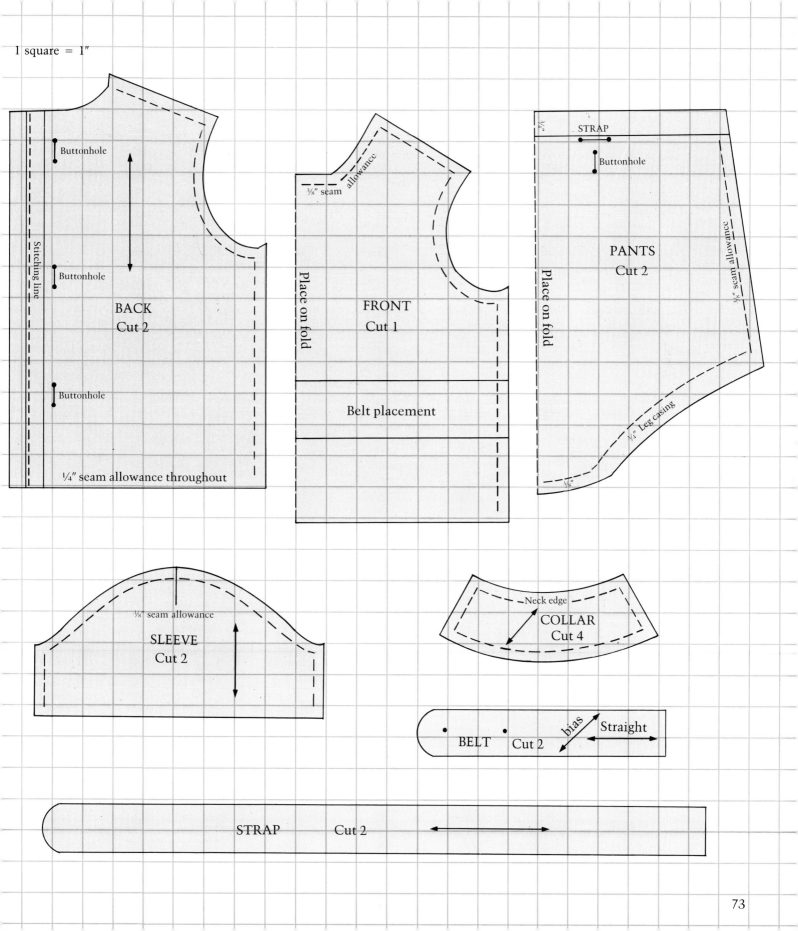

1 square = 1″

BACK
Cut 2

Buttonhole

Buttonhole

Buttonhole

Stitching line

¼″ seam allowance throughout

FRONT
Cut 1

⅜″ seam allowance

Place on fold

Belt placement

PANTS
Cut 2

STRAP

Buttonhole

Place on fold

⅜″ seam allowance

¼″ Leg casing

⅜″

SLEEVE
Cut 2

⅜″ seam allowance

COLLAR
Cut 4

Neck edge

BELT   Cut 2

bias   Straight

STRAP   Cut 2

Sailor Suit

Sailor Suit

Since Queen Mary ruled England, little children have been looking adorable (and sometimes self-conscious) in the classic sailor suit. Famous men of the recent past seem always to be wearing them in old family photographs showing the man as a boy. It is the dress-up, classic outfit, especially for a boy—more so, now, than even the Little Lord Fauntleroy velvet suit with the round-collared shirt used to be. And can't you imagine the old French watercolors and Impressionist paintings showing happy girls in braids skipping through a Sunday park wearing, of course, the classic sailor suit.

Like most classics, it is practical as well. This outfit is designed for easy movement and fit. The short-sleeved button-front top (you can put the buttons on either side) has side vents. The short pleated pants have adjustable button tucks in the waist and front, and elastic in the back. The sturdy fabric and the crisp colors make it perfect for visiting, nursery school, or family outings—the child can roughhouse and still look smart enough for company.

We made the sample in traditional colors—navy and white—but this suit would also be superb in deep red or strong pink.

Sailor suit pattern and instructions are for size 2. Measurements include ½" seam allowance. Pink, zig-zag, or overcast to finish all exposed seams.

Shop for these items

1½ yds. of 36" wide navy blue cotton or cotton-blend fabric.
½ yd of 36" wide white cotton or cotton-blend fabric.
⅝ yd. of 24" wide lightweight fusible interfacing.
5 buttons ½" wide.
18" of 1" wide elastic.
1½ yds. of ½" wide navy blue ribbon.
¾ yd. of ⅜" wide navy blue ribbon.
Sewing thread to match fabrics.
Dressmaker's carbon paper.
4 sheets of 18 x 24" tissue paper or tracing paper (to make paper pattern).

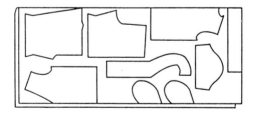

Cutting and marking the fabric

Enlarge pattern pieces shown on grid and trace onto tissue paper. Transfer all markings. Cut out paper pattern and pin to fabric, following the cutting layout for the navy blue pieces and placing the collar and cuff pieces on the straight grain of the white fabric. Transfer all markings from pattern pieces to fabric with dressmaker's carbon and cut out.

SAILOR PANTS

1. Sew center back crotch seam. Sew center front crotch seam.

2. Sew pockets to side seams at front and back of pants. Match notches. On pants front only edgestitch pockets.

3. Sew inseam.

4. Sew side seams and pockets.

5. Hem. Turn up 2" along hem fold line. Press. Fold in ¼". Blind-stitch in place.

6. Front of pant has pleat at waist. Fold pleat toward side seam of garment. Match notches at waist. Baste in place along waist stitching line.

7. With waistband flat, press up fold line edge ½″ toward wrong side of fabric. Sew the 2 ends of the waistband with right sides together at ½″, forming center back of waistband. Press allowance open. Place the right side of the center back of the waistband on the wrong side of the center back of the pants. Stitch along waistband stitching line.

8. Pull waistband up and over to right side of garment, placing pressed edge along stitching line. Topstitch in place

leaving a 2″ opening at center back. Insert elastic through opening. Pull and secure one end of elastic to line up with front pleat. Stitch with a vertical line of topstitching through waistband and elastic. If possible, check final fit of elastic (14″-17″) on child before securing opposite end the same way.

9. Topstitch center back opening.

10. Work buttonholes into waistband according to pattern markings. Sew on buttons.

This is a right side view of the finished pants, showing the front waistband and button fastening details. Two inverted pleats are formed down the front when the pants are buttoned. To accomodate growth, buttons can be left unfastened, and half of each inverted pleat will remain. See steps 6-8.

SAILOR TOP

1. Sew shoulder seams at ½″.

2. Attach ribbon to sleeve bands as pattern markings indicate.

3. Sew right side of sleeve band to wrong side of sleeve hem. Press allowances open, pulling band up to right side of sleeve. Fold band along fold line and edgestitch band to sleeve. Edgestitch hem of sleeve as well.

4. With garment flat, attach sleeve, matching sleeve notches to shoulder seam.

5. Stitch the 2 collar pieces, right sides together, leaving neck edge open. Trim seam allowances. Trim corners diagonally. Turn collar right side out. Press. Machine-baste neck edge of collar. Edgestitch collar.

6. Using pattern markings as guide, place ribbon onto collar ½″ from seamed edges. Miter ribbon at corners. Edgestitch ribbon in place.

7. Attach collar to body (wrong side of collar to right side of body), matching center back and shoulder notches. Sew at ½″.

8. Interface facing pieces. Sew together at center back. Press open seam allowance. Place facing onto garment with right sides together, matching center backs, shoulder notches, and center front edges. Sew at ½″. Trim seam allowances, notch curves, and trim corners diagonally. Turn facing to inside. Press. Finish raw edge by pressing back ¼″ to inside of facing and topstitching. Tack facing to shoulder seams.

9. Stitch side seams at ½″ up to side vent markings. Press open allowances. Hand-tack sleeve band allowances open.

10. Fold up hem along fold line; folding up side vent, facing, and hem allowance in one line. Turn in ¼″ and edgestitch. Fold facing back and tack to hem edge. Turn back ¼″ of the side seam vent allowance. Clip diagonally where side seam ends. Topstitch at ¼″.

11. Place buttons and buttonholes on fronts as pattern indicates.

Back view of finished top. The stripes are made by topstitching ribbon to the finished collar and cuffs. Note the mitered corner where the ribbon ends form an angle on the collar. See steps 2 and 6.

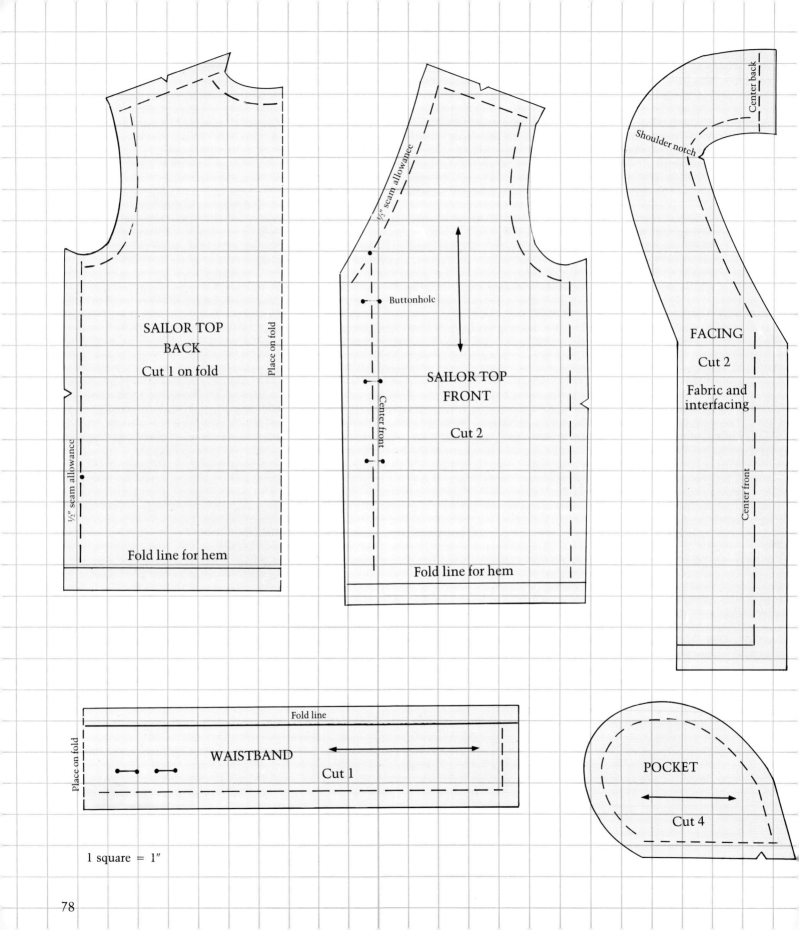

SAILOR TOP
BACK

Cut 1 on fold

Place on fold

½" seam allowance

Fold line for hem

½" seam allowance

Buttonhole

SAILOR TOP
FRONT

Cut 2

Center front

Fold line for hem

Shoulder notch

Center back

FACING

Cut 2

Fabric and
interfacing

Center front

Fold line

Place on fold

WAISTBAND

Cut 1

POCKET

Cut 4

1 square = 1"

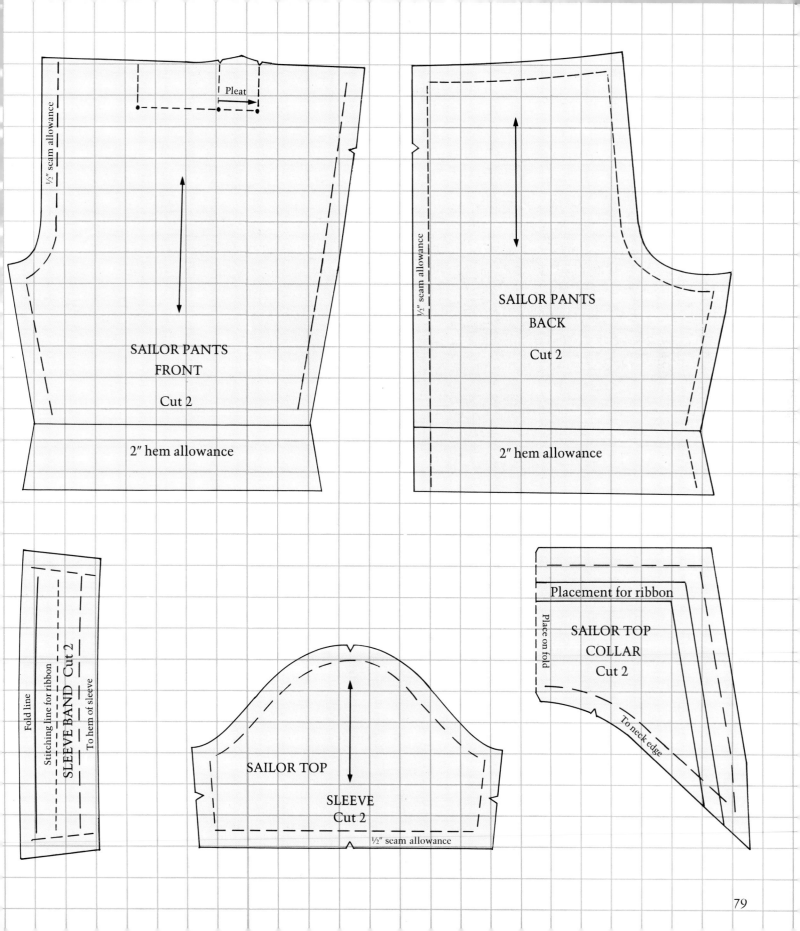

½" seam allowance

Pleat

SAILOR PANTS

FRONT

Cut 2

2" hem allowance

½" seam allowance

SAILOR PANTS

BACK

Cut 2

2" hem allowance

Fold line

Stitching line for ribbon

SLEEVE BAND Cut 2

To hem of sleeve

SAILOR TOP

SLEEVE

Cut 2

½" seam allowance

Placement for ribbon

Place on fold

SAILOR TOP

COLLAR

Cut 2

To neck edge

4.

Outdoor Outfits and Separates, mostly knitted and crocheted

Crocheted Layette Set

Blanket *Pullover*
Jacket *Overalls*
Cardigan *Bonnet*
Dress *Booties*
  Mittens

Layette is a word of French origin, meaning "an outfit of clothing for the newborn child."

As work on the layette is frequently started before the birth of the child, choice of color is not always simple. We used yellow and blue to make a set appropriate for either "boylet" or "girlette."

Deeply textured waffle stitch, made by alternating double crochet and post stitch, makes the warm, bulky fabric of blanket and jacket. Waffle stitch stripes add detail to the pullover, cardigan, dress, bonnet, and overalls.

The work for this complete set goes fast. Although the set totals nine separate items, no one of the nine is difficult to make. Since the full set will swathe every newborn inch in at least two layers of warm fabric, the infant is not likely to notice if you decide to skip one or two of the items altogether. The pullover, bonnet, thumbless mittens and booties with drawstrings would make an attractive mini-set.

The 28" square blanket can be used for "receiving" or as a carriage cover. The overalls have three-buttonhole, adjustable straps so that they can grow with the infant.

You may want to take the option of crocheting the buttons for all or some of the items, particularly those garments worn nearest the baby's skin. Soft, crocheted buttons can't press into the skin of a newborn lying on his/her back or tummy.

We designed and sized the layette set to fit a newborn to 6 months old baby. The finished chest measurement is 19".

Shop for these items

Sport-weight yarn to crochet the indicated gauge in 2 colors (we used yellow for MC, blue for CC) in 1¾ oz. (50 gr.) skeins.
For blanket, 6 skeins MC.
For jacket, 3 skeins MC.
For cardigan, dress, and pullover, 2 skeins MC for each piece.
For bonnet, 1 skein MC.
For booties and mittens, 1 skein MC for each pair.
For trimming all the above pieces, 1 skein CC.
For overalls, 2 skeins CC, 1 skein or ¼ oz. (7 gr.) MC.
For the entire set, 16 skeins MC, 3 skeins CC.
Crochet hook size F or size to give gauge, and steel crochet hook size 0.
18 ⅜" buttons (includes a few extra).

(Instructions for crocheted buttons, should you prefer them, are given at the end of the text.)

Correct gauge is important

Working in waffle st with larger size hk: 21 sts = 4", 12 rows = 4". Working in dc with larger size hk: 20 sts = 4", 11 rows 4". To ensure the correct finished measurements, take time to check gauge. Make a sample swatch: ch 23 for a waffle st swatch, 22 for a dc swatch, work the indicated number of rows for 4", fasten. Lay swatch flat and measure it—without bunching or stretching, swatch should be 4" square. If swatch is too small, try again with larger hk, if it is too large, try smaller hk.

Waffle stitch

Worked over an odd no. of sts. Make starting ch 2 sts longer than desired width.

Waffle foundation row: 1 dc in 4th ch from hk, 1 dc in each rem ch, ch 3, turn.

Waffle row 1: *Post st around 2nd dc (yo, insert hk through work from right side between first and 2nd dc, bring hk under 2nd dc and back through to right side between 2nd and 3rd dc; [yo and through

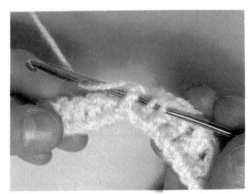

This shows a post stitch being made. The only difference between double crochet and post stitch is that in post stitch, the crochet hook is inserted through the crocheted fabric, underneath the "post" of a stitch of the previous row, instead of under the two top loops of the stitch.

2 lps on hook ÷ twice, 1 dc in next dc, rep from * across row, making last dc in top of turning ch, ch 3, turn.

Waffle row 2: *1 dc in 2nd st, post st around next st, rep from * to last st and turning ch (turning ch counts as 1 st), 1 dc in last st, 1 dc in top of turning ch, ch 3, turn. Rep Waffle rows 1 and 2 for waffle st.

Changing colors: This is the proper technique for making the CC waffle stripes on pullover, cardigan, dress, bonnet, and overalls. Work across to last st, yo, insert hk into st, yo and draw through 2 lps, drop color currently using, pick up new color, yo and draw through 2 lps. Ch 3, turn, and continue with new color, changing back to first color in same manner.

JACKET

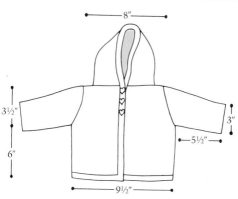

This is the front of the jacket, which is made entirely in ruggedly textured waffle stitch. We made only three buttonholes in the jacket edging, closing it at the neck, but you can space more buttonholes and buttons down the front edge if you prefer.

The back

With larger size hk and MC ch 51, work waffle foundation row—49 sts. Work in waffle st for 17 rows more.

Shape the armholes
Sl st across first 4 sts of next row, ch 3, work waffle st across to last 3 sts, ch 3, turn, leaving last 3 sts unworked—43 sts. Continue in waffle st for 8 rows more.

Shape the shoulders
Sl st across first 4 sts of next row, ch 3, work waffle st across to last 3 sts, ch 3, turn, leaving last 3 sts unworked—37 sts. Rep this row once—31 sts. Sl st across first 6 sts of next row, ch 3, work waffle st across to last 5 sts; fasten, leaving last 5 sts unworked—27 sts.

Right front

With larger size hk and MC ch 27, work foundation row—25 sts. Work waffle st until piece has same number of rows as back to armhole.

Shape the right armhole
Sl st across first 4 sts of next row, ch 3, work waffle st over rem sts, ch 3, turn—22 sts. Work waffle st for 6 rows more, ending at center front edge.

Shape the right front neck
Sl st across first 12 sts of next row, ch 3, work waffle st over rem sts, ch 3, turn—11 sts. Work 1 row more, ending at neck edge.

Shape the right shoulder
Work across to last 3 sts, ch 3, turn, leaving last 3 sts unworked—8 sts. Sl st across first 4 sts of next row, ch 3, waffle st over rem sts; fasten—5 sts.

Left front

Work same as right front to armhole.

Shape the left armhole
Waffle st across to last 3 sts, ch 3, turn, leaving last 3 sts unworked—22 sts. Work even until left armhole has same number of rows as right armhole, ending at armhole edge.

Shape the left front neck
Waffle st across to last 11 sts; ch 3, turn, leaving last 11 sts unworked—11 sts. Work 1 row more, ending at armhole edge.

Shape the left shoulder
Sl st across first 4 sts of next row, ch 3, waffle st over rem sts, ch 3, turn—8 sts. Waffle st across to last 3 sts of next row; fasten, leaving last 3 sts unworked—5 stitches.

The sleeve

With larger size hk and MC ch 31, work waffle foundation row—29 sts. Work waffle st, inc 1 st at each end of 2nd row and rep inc every 3rd row twice more—35 sts. Work even until sleeve is 16 rows from beg.

Shape the sleeve cap
Sl st across first 4 sts of next row, ch 3, waffle st across to last 3 sts; ch 3, turn, leaving last 3 sts unworked—29 sts. Rep this row twice more, fasten—17 sts. Make 2 sleeves.

The hood

With larger size hk and MC ch 61, work waffle foundation row—59 sts. Work waffle st for 13 rows more, fasten; turn.

Back of hood

Sk first 20 sts of next row, join MC to 21st st, ch 3, work waffle st over next 18 sts, ch 3, turn, leaving last 20 sts unworked—19 sts. Work 1 row even. Dec 1 st at each end of next row—17 sts. Work 2 rows even. Rep these 3 rows once more, fasten—15 sts. With tapestry needle and MC, sew edges of hood back to unworked sts at either end of 14th row.

Hood edging

With right side facing and smaller size hk, join MC to one corner of hood, 2 sc in corner, 2 sc in each row end around lower (neck) edge of hood, 2 sc in opposite corner, fasten.

Finishing the garment

With tapestry needle and MC, join shoulder seams. Set in sleeves, then join side and sleeve seams. Join lower edge of hood to neck opening.
Jacket edging.
Rnd 1: With right side facing and smaller size hk, join CC to lower edge by right side seam. Working along opposite side of foundation ch, 1 sc in each st to lower right front corner, 3 sc in corner, 2 sc in each row end along right front edge to hood joining, 1 sc in each st around hood to left front, 2 sc in each row end along left front edge to lower corner, 3 sc in corner, 1 sc in each rem st around lower edge; join with sl st, ch 1, do not turn.
Rnd 2: 1 sc in each sc around, evenly spacing 3 buttonholes down one of the fronts (to make buttonhole, ch 3, sk 1 st) with top buttonhole at neck edge; join at end of rnd, ch 1, do not turn.
Rnd 3: Sl st in each sc and in each buttonhole ch around, join; fasten.
Sew on buttons opposite buttonholes.

The back

With smaller size hk and MC ch 47. 1 sc in 2nd ch from hk, 1 sc in each rem ch, ch 1, turn—46 sc. Work 5 rows sc, ch 3, turn. Change to larger size hk, work 1 dc in each st of next row, change to CC at end of row. Waffle stripe: Work waffle rows 1 and 2, change to MC at end of 2nd row. Work in dc for 11 rows or until desired length to armhole.

Shape the armholes

Sl st across first 4 sts of next row, ch 3, 1 dc in each st across to last 3 sts, ch 3, turn, leaving last 3 sts unworked—40 sts. Work 7 dc rows more, fasten.

Left front

With smaller size hk and MC, ch 24. Work same as cardigan back to armhole—23 sts.

Shape the left armhole

Sl st across first 4 sts of next row, ch 3, dc to end, ch 3, turn—20 sts. Work 4 dc rows more, ending at center front edge.

CARDIGAN

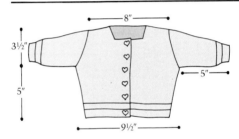

Shape the left front neck

Sl st across first 11 sts of next row, ch 3, dc to end, ch 3, turn—10 sts. Work 2 dc rows more, fasten.

Right front

Work same as left front to armhole.

Shape the right armhole

Dc across next row to last 3 sts, ch 3, turn, leaving last 3 sts unworked—20 sts. Work 4 dc rows more, ending at armhole edge.

Shape the right front neck

Dc across next row to last 10 sts, ch 3, turn, leaving last 10 sts unworked—10 sts. Work 2 dc rows more, fasten.

The sleeve

With smaller size hk and MC, ch 28. Work border and waffle stripe same as for cardigan back—27 sts. Change to larger size hk and work dc, inc 1 st at each end of first dc row. Rep inc every 3rd row 3 times more—35 sts.

Shape the sleeve cap

Sl st across first 4 sts of next row, ch 3, dc across to last 3 sts, ch 3, turn, leaving last 3 sts unworked—29 sts. Rep this row twice more, fasten—17 sts.

Finishing the garment

With tapestry needle and MC, sew shoulder seams. Set in sleeves, then sew side and sleeve seams.

Neck edging

With right side facing and smaller size hk, join MC to first st at right center front neck, 1 sc in each st and 2 sc in each row end around neck edge, ch 1, turn. Work 2 sc rows more, fasten.

Button border

With right side facing and smaller size hk, join MC to corner of one center front edge (depending whether you want buttons on the right or left front edge), *1 sc in first row end, 2 sc in next row end, rep from * along edge, ch 1, turn. Work 2 sc rows more, fasten.
Note: Check size of buttonhole by slipping a button through. If opening is too small, make a ch-2 space instead of ch-1 for each buttonhole.

Buttonhole border

Work first row same as for button band. Make 6 evenly spaced buttonholes along next row—(ch 1, sk 1 st) for each buttonhole. 1 sc into each st and each buttonhole ch for last row, fasten. Sew on buttons opposite buttonholes.

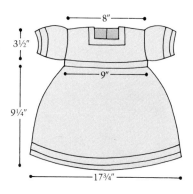

DRESS

This is the dress, seen from the back. The front and back yokes are made first and joined at the sides. The skirt is then worked from the lower edge of the yoke to the hem, and seamed down the back. The fullness of the skirt is created by doubling the number of stitches across one row. Note also the button closure, set-in sleeve, and contrasting-color waffle stitch stripes.

Dress body is crocheted in four pieces—first the front and back yokes are made and joined at the sides, then the skirt is worked from the lower edge of the yoke and seamed down the back.

Front yoke
With smaller size hk and MC, ch 47, 1 sc in 2nd ch from hk, 1 sc in each rem ch, ch 3, turn—46 sts. Change to larger size hk and work 1 row dc, change to CC at end of row. Waffle stripe: Work waffle rows 1 and 2, change to MC at end of 2nd row. Work 1 row sc, ch 1, turn, ready for a wrong side row.

Shape the armholes
Sl st across first 4 sts of next row, ch 3, dc across to last 3 sts, ch 3, turn, leaving last 3 sts unworked—40 sts. Work 4 dc rows more.

Shape the left front neck
Work across first 9 sts of next row (10 sts including turning ch), turn. Work 2 dc rows more, fasten, do not turn.

Shape the right front neck
With right side facing, skip 20 sts of last long row for center front neck, join MC to 21st st, ch 3, dc in rem 9 sts, ch 3, turn. Work 2 dc rows more, fasten.

Right back yoke
With larger size hk and MC, ch 23, work same as front yoke to armhole—22 sts.

Shape the armhole
Sl st across first 4 sts of next row, ch 3, dc in rem sts, ch 3, turn—19 sts. Work 7 dc rows, fasten.

Left back yoke
Work same as right back yoke to armhole.

Shape the armhole
Dc across to last 3 sts of next row, ch 3, turn, leaving last 3 sts unworked—19 sts. Work 7 dc rows, fasten. With tapestry needle and MC, sew shoulder and side seams of yoke sections.

The skirt
With right side of work facing and larger size hk, working along opposite side of foundation chain, join MC to first st at lower edge of right back yoke, ch 3, work 2 dc in each rem st of lower yoke edge across to last st, 1 dc in last st, ch 3, turn—178 sts. Work even in dc until skirt measures 8¼", end ready for a right side row, change to CC at end of last row. Waffle stripe: Work waffle rows 1 and 2, change to MC at end of 2nd row. Work 2 sc rows, fasten.

The sleeve
With smaller size hk and MC, ch 28, 1 sc in 2nd ch from hk, 1 sc in each rem ch, ch 1, turn. Work 1 sc row more, ch 3, turn—27 sts. Change to larger size hk, dc across next row, inc every other st, change to CC at end of row—40 sts. Work waffle stripe as for front yoke, change to MC at end of 2nd row, ch 3, turn. Dc across next row, dec 5 sts evenly spaced, ch 1, turn—35 sts. Work 4 dc rows even.

Shape the sleeve cap
Sl st across first 4 sts of next row, ch 3, dc across to last 3 sts, ch 3, turn, leaving last 3 sts unworked—29 sts. Rep this row twice more, fasten—17 sts.

Finishing the garment
Neck border: With right side facing and smaller size hk, join MC to first st of left neck edge at center back, 1 sc in each st and 2 sc in each row end around neck edge, ch 1, turn. Work 2 sc rows more, fasten.

Button border: With right side facing and smaller size hk, join MC to end of first row of right back neck, 1 sc in each row end to beg of skirt, ch 1, turn. Work 2 sc rows more, fasten.

Buttonhole border: With right side facing and smaller size hk, join MC to left back opening above beg of skirt, 1 sc in each row end to left back neck, ch 1, turn. Sc across next row, working 4 evenly spaced buttonholes (ch 1, sk 1 st for buttonhole), ch 1, turn. 1 sc in each st and each buttonhole ch across for last row, fasten.

With tapestry needle and MC, set in sleeves, sew sleeve seams and center back skirt seam, positioning buttonhole border to overlap button border. Sew buttons opposite buttonholes.

PULLOVER

This close-up shows the shoulder neck edge of the pullover, unbuttoned. The last 2 rows of the back shoulder overlap the front shoulder for the decorative button fastening.

The back

With smaller size hk and MC, ch 47, 1 sc in 2nd ch from hk, 1 sc in each rem ch, ch 1, turn—46 sts. Work 5 sc rows, ch 3, turn. Change to larger size hk, work 1 row dc, change to CC at end of row, ch 3, turn. Waffle stripe: Work waffle rows 1 and 2, change to MC at end of 2nd row. Work 11 dc rows, or until desired length to armhole.

Shape the armholes
Sl st across first 4 sts of next row, ch 3, dc across to last 3 sts, ch 3, turn, leaving last 3 sts unworked—40 sts. Work 7 dc rows more.

Shape the right back neck
Dc in first 12 sts of next row (13 sts including turning ch), 1 hdc in next st, 1 sc in next st, sl st in next st, fasten, turn. Sk the sl st, sc, and hdc, join yarn to first dc, ch 1, 1 sc in next st, 1 hdc in next st, dc across rem 10 sts, fasten.

Shape the left back neck
With right side facing, sk center 8 dc of last long row, join MC to 9th dc, 1 sc in next st, 1 hdc in next st, dc across rem 13 sts, ch 3, turn. Dc in first 9 sts of next

row (10 sts including turning ch), 1 hdc in next st, 1 sc in next st, sl st in next st, fasten.

Back neck edging: With right side facing and smaller size hk, join MC to first st at armhole edge, ch 1, work 1 sc in each st across entire edge, making a buttonhole at center of each shoulder edge (ch 2, sk 1 st for buttonhole), ch 1, turn. Sl st in each st and each buttonhole ch across, fasten.

The front

Work same as back until armhole is 5 rows deep.

Shape the right front neck
Dc across first 12 sts of next row—13 sts including turning ch; 1 hdc in next st, 1 sc in next st, sl st in next st, fasten, turn. Sk sl st, sc, and hdc, join MC to first dc, ch 1, 1 sc in next st, 1 hdc in next st, dc across rem 10 sts, ch 3, turn. Dc across first 6 sts of next row—7 sts including turning ch; 1 hdc in next st, 1 sc in next st, sl st in next st, fasten.

Shape the left front neck
With wrong side facing, sk center 8 dc of last long row, join MC to 9th dc, ch 1, sl

st in next st, 1 sc in next st, 1 hdc in next st, dc across rem 13 sts, ch 3, turn. Dc across first 9 sts of next row—10 sts including turning ch; 1 hdc in next st, 1 sc in next st, sl st in next st, fasten, turn. Sk sl st, sc, and hdc, join MC to first dc, ch 1, 1 sc in next st, 1 hdc in next st, dc across rem 7 sts, fasten.

Front neck edging: With right side facing and smaller size hk, join MC to first st at armhole edge, work 1 sc in each st across entire edge. Work 1 row even, fasten.

Sleeves

Work in the same manner as cardigan sleeves.

Finishing the garment

Pin back and front shoulders so that last 2 dc rows and buttonhole edging of back overlap front (right sides out). With tapestry needle and MC, set in sleeves, sewing through both thicknesses of fabric at shoulder overlap. Sew side and sleeve seams. Sew buttons to front shoulders opposite buttonholes.

Step 1. Single crochet

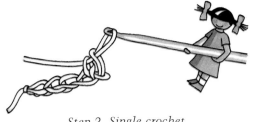

Step 2. Single crochet

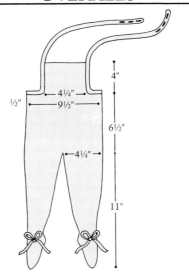

A rear view of the overalls shows the short rows used to shape the pants seat. Short rows are made by working only partway across a number of consecutive rows to build up the fabric in one area. When short rows are completed, all the stitches are worked across from end to end, giving a smooth edge to the work.

Overalls are made in 2 flat pieces, one front and one back, starting at top edge, working towards feet.

The front bib

With smaller size hk and CC, ch 23 for top edge of bib, 1 sc in 2nd ch from hk, 1 sc in each rem ch, ch 3, turn—22 sts. Change to larger size hk and dc across, changing to MC at end of row. Waffle stripe: Work waffle rows 1 and 2, change to CC at end of 2nd row. Work 8 dc rows, fasten, turn.

Tummy section

With larger size hk and CC, ch 12, yo, insert hk into first st of last bib row, dc across lower edge of bib, ch 15, turn. 1 dc in 4th ch from hk, 1 dc in each of rem 10 ch, dc across bib, 1 dc in each of 12 ch, ch 3, turn—46 sts (22 across lower edge of bib, 12 sts on each side of bib). Work 17 dc rows.

First leg

Dc first 22 sts of next row—23 sts including turning ch; ch 5, turn. 1 dc in 4th ch from hk, 1 dc in next ch, dc across rem sts, ch 3, turn—26 sts. Dec 1 st at inside leg edge on each of next 2 rows, then work 1 row even—24 sts. Rep these 3 rows 5 times more—14 sts.

Make eyelets for ankle drawstring: 1 dc in first st of next row, *ch 1, sk 1 st,

1 dc in next st, rep from * across, ch 3, turn. Dc in each st and each ch-1 sp for next row, ch 3, turn—14 sts.

Shape the instep: Dec 1 st at inside leg edge on next row, work 1 row even—13 sts. Rep these 2 rows once—12 sts. Dec 1 st at each end of next row, fasten—10 sts.

Second leg

With larger size hk and CC, ch 2, 1 dc in st of last long row nearest inside edge of first leg, dc across rem 22 sts, ch 3, turn—23 sts. Dc in each st and each ch for next row, ch 3, turn—26 sts. Dec 1 st at inside leg edge on each of next 2 rows, work 1 row even—24 sts. Rep these 3 rows 5 times more—14 sts. Make eyelets and shape instep same as first leg, fasten.

The back

With smaller size hk and CC, ch 48, 1 dc in 4th ch from hk, 1 dc in each rem ch, ch 3, turn—46 sts. Change to larger size hk.

Shape the pants seat

Row 1: Dc across next row to last 7 sts, 1 hdc in next st, 1 sc in next st, ch 1, turn.
Row 2-6: 1 sc in first st, 1 hdc in next st, dc across to last 7 sts, 1 hdc in next st, 1 sc in next st, ch 1, turn. Rep this row 4 times more.

Row 7: 1 sc in first st, 1 hdc in next st, dc to end, ch 3, turn.
Row 8-11: Work 3 dc rows across all sts—46 sts.

Legs

Work first and second leg same as front legs to completion of eyelet rows, fasten—14 sts. With tapestry needle and CC, sew side and leg seams.

Left foot

With right side facing and larger size hk, join CC to end of first instep row of left front leg, ch 3, 1 dc in same row end, *1 dc in next row end, 2 dc in next row end, rep from * once, 1 dc in each of the 6 sts of last instep row (toe edge), **2 dc in next row end, 1 dc in next row end, rep from ** twice, dc in each of the 14 dc along last row of left back leg, ch 3, turn—37 dc. Work 2 dc rows, fasten.

Right foot

With right side facing and larger size hk, join CC to first of 14 dc along last row of right back leg, ch 3, dc in rem 13 dc; working along row ends of right front instep, *1 dc in first row end, 2 dc in next row end, rep from * twice, dc in each of the 6 sts of last instep row (toe edge), **2 dc in next row end, 1 dc in next row end, rep from ** once, 2 dc in next row end, ch 3, turn. Work 2 dc rows, fasten. With tapestry needle and CC, sew foot seams.

Finishing the garment

Straps

With smaller size hk and CC, ch 60; with right side of bib facing, 2 sc in end of top row at right edge of bib, 1 sc in next row end, *2 sc in next row end, 1 sc in next row end, rep from * along bib edge; working along opposite side of foundation ch, 1 sc in each st along side and back edges to left edge of bib; **2 sc in next row end, 1 sc in next row end, rep from ** along bib edge; ch 61, turn. 1 sc in 2nd ch from hk, 1 sc in each ch and in each st around , ch 1, turn.

Buttonhole row: Sc in first 2 sts of next row, *ch 2, sk 2 sts, sc in next 3 sts, rep from * twice more, sc across to last 14 sts, rep from * 3 times, ending last rep with 2 sc, ch 1, turn—3 buttonholes in each strap end. Sc in each sc and each buttonhole ch for next row, fasten. Sew 2 buttons to outside top edge of back, about 3" from side seams.

Ankle drawstrings: With smaller size hk and MC, make 2 ch about 20" long, fasten. Thread through ankle eyelets.

BONNET

This is the bonnet, seen from the back. The bonnet is crocheted flat, in a "T" shape. The free stitches along the lower edge of the horizontal part of the T are joined to the row ends of the vertical section, creating a three-dimensional curved shape that conforms well to a baby's head.

With larger size hk and MC, ch 61, 1 sc in 2nd ch from hk, 1 sc in each rem ch, ch 1, turn—60 sts. Work 1 row sc, ch 3, turn. Work 1 row dc, change to CC at end of row. Waffle stripe: Work waffle rows 1 and 2, change to MC at end of 2nd row. Work 13 dc rows, fasten, turn.

Back of bonnet

Sk first 20 sts of last row, join MC to 21st st, ch 3, dc across next 19 sts, turn, leaving last 20 sts unworked. Work 3 dc rows, dec 1 st at each end of next row, rep dec every 3rd row twice more (10 rows worked), fasten. With tapestry needle and MC, sew edges of bonnet back to unworked sts at either end of last long row.

Bonnet border

With right side facing and smaller size hk, join MC to first st of first row of bonnet; working along opposite side of foundation ch, 3 sc in first (corner) st, 1 sc in each st to next corner, 3 sc in last st; *1 sc in next row end, 2 sc in next row end, rep from * to first bonnet back seam, 1 sc in each st along bonnet back edge to second back seam; **1 sc in next row end, 2 sc in next row end, rep from ** to corner, join with sl st, ch 4, turn.

Make eyelets for bonnet drawstring: Sk first 2 sts of next row, *1 hdc in next st, ch 1, sk 1 st, rep from *, ending with 1 sc in last st, fasten.

Bonnet drawstring: With smaller size hk and CC, make a ch about 45" long, fasten. Thread through eyelets.

Chain stitch

BOOTIES

A side view of one bootie. The stitches of the sole are worked into the row ends around the instep and heel. The contrasting-color lace is made of chain stitch and threaded through eyelets.

First bootie

With larger size hk and MC, ch 30, 1 sc in 2nd ch from hk, 1 sc in each rem ch, ch 3, turn—29 sts. Work 6 dc rows, ch 4 at end of last row, turn. Make eyelets for ankle drawstrings: Sk first 2 sts of next row, 1 dc in next st, *ch 1, sk 1 st, 1 dc in next st, rep from * to end, ch 3, turn. Dc in each st and in each ch-1 sp across for next row, ch 3, turn—28 sts.

Shape the instep

Dec 1 st at beg of next row, dc in next 8 sts, dec 1 st, 1 dc in next st, turn, leaving 14 sts unworked—12 sts. Mark the point between the 7th and 8th st of the unworked 14 sts for center back heel (to be worked later). Work 1 dc row even, dec 1 st at each end of next row—10 sts. Rep these 2 rows once more—8 sts. Rep dec row once more—6 sts.

Shape heel and sole

With right side facing and larger size hk, join MC to first instep row at end farthest from unworked sts of last long row, ch 3, 1 dc in first row end, *1 dc in next row end, 2 dc in next row end, rep from * once, dc across 6 sts of last instep row (toe edge), **2 dc in next row end, 1 dc in next row end, rep from ** twice, dc across 14 heel sts, ch 3, turn—37 sts. Work 2 dc rows, fasten.

Second bootie

Work same as first bootie until eyelet rows have been completed, fasten, turn.

Shape instep

Sk first 14 sts of next row, join MC to 15th st, ch 3, dec 1 st, dc across next 8 sts, dec 1 st, 1 dc in turning ch, ch 3, turn. Mark the point between the 7th and 8th st of the 14 skipped sts for center heel. Work dec rows same as for instep of first bootie.

Shape heel and sole

Join MC to fasten-off point of 14 skipped sts, ch 3, dc across next 13 sts to instep, *1 dc in next row end, 2 dc in next row end, rep from * twice more, dc across 6 sts of last instep row for toe edge, **2 dc in next row end, 1 dc in next row end, rep from ** once more, 2 dc in next row end, ch 3, turn. Work 2 dc rows, fasten.

With tapestry needle and MC, sew side leg seams. Fold each bootie in half with heel marker at center back, and sew up soles. Bootie ankle drawstrings: With smaller size hk and CC, make 2 ch about 22" long, fasten. Thread drawstrings through eyelets.

BLANKET

With larger size hk and MC ch 151, work waffle foundation row—149 sts. Work waffle st until blanket is 84 rows long, or desired length; fasten.

Blanket edging: With smaller size hk, working along opposite side of foundation ch, join CC to first st, 1 sc in each st to corner, 3 sc in corner; working along row ends, alternate (2 sc in first row end, 1 sc in next row end) to corner, 3 sc in corner; working along last waffle st row, 1 sc in each st, 3 sc in corner; work along rem row ends as for opposite edge; 3 sc in last corner, join with sl st. Fasten.

MITTENS

Work mitten same as bootie until first eyelet row has been completed. Dc in each st and each ch-1 sp for next row, working last st into 3rd st of turning ch-4, ch 3, turn—29 sts. Work 4 dc rows.

Dec row: Dec 1 st at beg of next row, dc across next 9 sts, dec 1 st, 1 dc in next st, dec 1 st, dc across next 9 sts, dec 1 st, 1 dc in turning ch, ch 3, turn—25 sts. Rep dec row, having 7 sts between dec—21 sts. Rep dec row once more, having 5 sts between dec, fasten—17 sts. Fold mittens in half. With tapestry needle and MC, sew seams.

Mitten drawstrings: Make mitten drawstrings same as bootie ankle drawstrings. Thread through eyelets.

CROCHETED BUTTONS

You may prefer to crochet all or some of the buttons for the layette, instead of purchasing them. Crocheted buttons have several good features—being made of the same fiber as the garment, they rarely fall off; being flexible, they don't stretch the buttonholes or fray them; being soft, they don't poke into flesh.

With smaller size hk, ch 2, leaving a 6" length of yarn for sewing; 6 sc in 2nd ch from hk, join with sl st, do not turn, sl st in front lp of each st around, fasten, cut yarn leaving another 6" length for sewing. Pull yarn ends through to back of button.

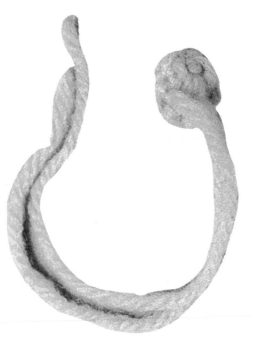

Crocheted Angora Sacque with Lustrous Highlights

hat the French call a "sacque" is simply a short peasant's cloak that fastens at the throat. In our interpretation for an infant, it has become a crocheted, straight-silhouette, raglan cardigan, with bloused sleeves, a delicate picot edging, and sewn-in ribbon ties at the neck. The yoke is formed with alternate rows of single and double crochet, with decorative shell stitch worked below it.

This unusual design is copied from a similar sacque that has been passed down through the generations in the author's native Sweden. It contrasts two fibers rarely found together in the same sweater—fuzzy, off-white, angora-wool and stark, shiny-white, mercerized cotton. Both you and your baby will enjoy the feel and the look of these contrapuntal effects—the shiny-matteness, the fuzzy-slickness, and the white-on-whiteness.

Since the pattern is simply a striped cardigan, a very different-looking sweater from the one pictured can be produced by substituting yarns. For a sporty look, use a flat-textured wool in strongly contrasting colors, add buttonloops, and sew on buttons.

When you shop for the angora wool, be sure the fibers are not so long or so loose that a baby could pluck them free and put them in its mouth.

Directions are written for 6 months size with changes for 12, 18, and 24 months sizes in parentheses. The finished chest measurements are 22 (24, 26, 28)".

Shop for these items

Fluffy baby or fingering yarn, 3 (3, 4, 4,) 1¾ oz (50 gr) balls (we used an off-white wool and angora blend).

Mercerized cotton, size 3, 11 (11, 14, 14) yd skeins and size 5, 1 (1, 1, 1) yd skein (we used white).

Steel crochet hook size 4, or size to give gauge.

Two ¼" ribbons, about 24" long.

Note: The thinner cotton is used only to crochet the picot edgings.

Correct gauge is important

8 shells = 4", 18 shell st rows = 4". To ensure the correct finished measurements, take time to check gauge. Make a sample swatch: ch 36, 1 sc in 2nd st from hk, 1 sc in each rem ch, ch 3, turn. Work 18 rows shell stitch (see directions below), fasten. Lay swatch flat and measure it—without bunching or stretching, swatch should be 4" square. If swatch is too small, try again with a larger hk—if it is too big, try a smaller hk.

Shell stitch

This stitch is worked over a multiple of 4 + 3 sts.

Shell foundation row: (wrong side)—*sk 3 sts, (2 dc, ch 1, 2 dc) in next st, rep from * to last 3 sts, sk 2 sts, 1 dc in last st, ch 3, turn.

Shell pattern row: (2 dc, ch 1, 2 dc) in each ch-1 sp across, end ch 1, 1 dc in top st of turning ch, ch 3, turn. Rep pattern row.

Changing yarns: This is the proper technique for changing back and forth between the fluffy yarn and the cotton

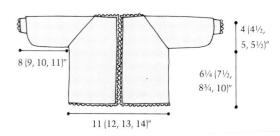

8 (9, 10, 11)"
11 (12, 13, 14)"
4 (4½, 5, 5½)"
6¼ (7½, 8¾, 10)"

yarn. Work across to last st, yo, insert hk into st, yo and draw through 2 lps, cut yarn currently using, pick up new yarn, yo and draw through 2 lps. Ch 3, turn, and continue with new yarn.

Leave ends about 2" long when you cut and join yarns. Crochet over the ends as you start the next row, and you will save having to weave them in later.

Sacque body

With fluffy yarn, ch 180 (196, 212, 228), 1 sc in 2nd ch from hk, 1 sc in each rem ch, ch 3, turn—179 (195, 211, 227) sts. Work shell foundation row—44 (48, 52, 56) shells with ch 3 at beg of row, 1 dc at end of row. Work 3 shell pat rows, change to cotton yarn at end of last row, ch 3, turn. *Work 1 pat row, change to fluffy yarn at end of row, ch 3, turn. Work 4 pat rows, change to cotton yarn at end of last row, ch 3, turn. Rep from * until piece measures about 6¼ (7½, 8¾, 10)" from beg, or desired length from underarm to lower edge, fasten.

The yoke

Right front

With right side of work facing, working along opposite side of foundation ch, join fluffy yarn to first st, ch 2, 1 dc in same st, 1 dc in each of the next 40 (45, 45, 51) sts, change to cotton yarn at end of row, ch 1, turn, leaving rem 138 (149, 165, 176) sts unworked—41 (45, 46, 52) sts.

Dec row 1: Draw up a lp in each of first 2 sts, yo, draw hk through all 3 lps on hk for dec, 1 sc in each rem st, end with 1 sc in top of turning ch, changing to fluffy yarn at end of row, ch 2, turn—40 (45, 45, 51) sts.

Dec row 2: Dc across, sk last st for dec, changing to cotton yarn at end of row, ch 2, turn—39 (44, 44, 50) sts.

Rep dec rows 1 and 2, taking off one st at raglan armhole edge each row, until 17 (19, 16, 18) sts rem. Right front yoke should measure about 4 (4½, 5, 5½)" from underarm and be 24 (27, 30, 33) rows deep. Fasten.

Left front

With right side of work facing, working along opposite side of foundation ch, join

The upper right section of the sacque front shows the raglan seam joining and the picot edge in detail. The stripes all meet at the raglan seams almost at right angles, which gives the design a pretty continuity all around the yoke. Each picot is formed

fluffy yarn 41 (46, 46, 51) sts from end, ch 2, 1 dc in same st, 1 dc in each of rem 40 (45, 45, 50) sts changing to cotton yarn at end of row, ch 1, turn—41 (46, 46, 51) sts.

Dec row 1: Sc across, sk last st for dec, changing to fluffy yarn at end of row, ch 2, turn—40 (45, 45, 51) sts.

Dec row 2: Draw up a lp in first st, yo, draw up a lp in next st, yo and through all 4 lps on hk for dec, dc across rem sts, changing to cotton yarn at end of row, ch 2, turn—39 (44, 44, 50) sts.

Rep dec rows 1 and 2, taking off one st at raglan armhole edge each row, until 17 (19, 16, 18) sts rem. Fasten. Left front yoke should be 24 (27, 30, 33) rows deep and should mirror the right front.

Yoke back

With right side of work facing, working along rem sts of foundation ch between

by making a short chain and doubling the
chain back on itself with a slip stitch.

left and right front, sk 9 (9, 12, 12) sts
from right front raglan armhole edge,
join fluffy yarn in 10th (10th, 13th, 13th)
st, ch 2, 1 dc in each of next 78 (84, 94,
100) sts, change to cotton yarn at end of
row, ch 2, turn, leaving 9 (9, 12, 11) sts
unworked betweeen back and left front
raglan armhole edge—79 (85, 95, 101) sts.

Dec row 1: Draw up a lp in each of first 2
sts, yo, draw hk through all 3 lps on hk
for dec, sc across, sk last st for dec,

changing to fluffy yarn at end of row, ch
2, turn—77 (83, 93, 99) sts.
Dec row 2: Draw up a lp in first st, yo,
draw up a lp in next st, yo and through
all 4 lps on hk for dec, dc across, sk last
st for dec, changing to cotton yarn at end
of row, ch 2, turn—75 (81, 91, 97) sts.

Rep dec rows, taking off one st at each
armhole edge every row, until 31 (31, 35,
35) sts rem, fasten. Back yoke should be
same depth and number of rows as left
and right front yoke.

The sleeve

Beg at underarm, with fluffy yarn ch 72
(80, 88, 92), 1 sc in 2nd ch from hk, 1 sc
in each rem ch, ch 3, turn—71 (79, 87,
91) sts. Work shell foundation row—17
(19, 21, 22) shells with ch 3 at beg of row,
1 dc at end of row. Work 3 shell pat rows,
change to cotton yarn at end of last row,
ch 3, turn. *Work 1 pat row, change to
fluffy yarn at end of row, ch 3, turn. Work
4 pat rows, change to cotton yarn at end
of last row, ch 3, turn. Rep from * until
sleeve measures 5½ (6, 7, 8)", or desired
length from underarm to wrist, less 2½
(3, 3, 3)", ch 1 at end of last row, turn.
Dec row: Sl st across first 5 sts, ch 2,
work shell pat in next 15 (17, 19, 20)
shells, sk last shell, ch 1, 1 dc in last dc
of last shell, ch 1, turn. Rep dec row 1 (2,
2, 2) times, ch 2, turn—13 (13, 15, 16)
shells.

Cuff

Row 1: 1 dc in each of first 2 dc, sk ch-1
sp, *1 dc in each of next 2 dc, sk ch-1 sp,
1 dc in each of next 2 dc, rep from *
across all shells, ch 1, turn.
Row 2: Sc across, ch 2, turn.
Row 3: Dc across, ch 1, turn.
Repeat rows 2 and 3 once, then rep row
2 once, fasten.

Sleeve cap

With right side of sleeve facing, working
along opposite side of foundation ch, sk
first 5 (5, 6, 6) sts, join fluffy yarn to 6th
(6th, 7th, 7th) st, ch 2, dc across to last 6
(6, 7, 7) sts, change to cotton yarn at end
of row, ch 1, turn; leaving last (6, 7, 7) sts
unworked—61 (69, 75, 79) sts.

Single crochet

Dec row 1: Draw up a lp in each of first 2
sts, yo and through all 3 lps on hk for dec,
sc across row, sk last st for dec, change
to fluffy yarn at end of row, ch 1,
turn—59 (67, 73, 77) sts.
Dec row 2: Draw up a lp in first st, yo,
draw up a lp in next st, yo and through
all 4 lps on hk for dec, dc across row, sk
last st for dec, change to cotton yarn at
end of row, ch 1, turn—57 (65, 71, 75) sts.

Rep dec rows until 13 (15, 15, 13) sts rem,
fasten. Sleeve cap should be same depth
and number of rows as front and back
yokes.

Finishing the garment

With tapestry needle and yarn, sew raglan and sleeve seams, taking care to
match the stripes.

Outer edging: With right side of work
facing, join thinner cotton to lower edge
below right underarm, ch 1, 1 sc in same
st; 1 sc in each st and in each ch-1 sp, 3
sc in each corner st along outer edge, join
with sl st, ch 1, do not turn.

Picot rnd: *Sl st across next 3 sts, (ch
3, sl st in first ch of ch 3 for picot),* rep
betw *'s to lower right corner, 3 sc in
corner st, rep betw *'s up right front edge
to beg of yoke, (ch 4, sk 2 sc, sl st in each
of next 3 sts for ribbon opening) rep betw
*'s to 1" from neck edge, rep ribbon
opening, rep betw *'s around neck opening with 3 sc in each corner st, finish
outer edge in same manner, working 2
ribbon openings on left front yoke edge
opposite the first 2. Join with sl st, fasten.

Sleeve edging: With right side of work
facing, join thinner cotton to one sleeve
cuff edge near seam, *sl st across next 3
sts, picot, rep from * around, join with
sl st, fasten. Edge other sleeve in same
manner.

Knitted Yoke
of Hearts

Knitted Yoke of Hearts

This snug set—sweater, hat, and long socks—is knitted with fine fingering wool in the practical, straightforward colors of the outdoor mountain life. It will keep your child warm on nippy days, and the red hearts will make the grownups smile.

The button fastening at the left shoulder makes the sweater easy to pull on and off. The socks are knee-high, with firm ribbings to keep them up. Though the depth of the hat can be varied, it is designed to cover the ears completely, as is a seaman's watch cap.

The knitted-in ♥ panels are meticulously stranded with the yarns overlapped at every stitch. This refined touch of the loving needle-artist's hand will be noticeable to the discerning eye, because the work lies uniformly flat.

Instructions are for 6 months size. Changes for 12 months, 18 months, and 24 months sizes are in parentheses. Finished chest measurements are 22 (23, 25, 28)".

Shop for these items

Baby or fingering yarn to knit the indicated gauge in 3 colors (we used grey for MC, red for ♥ , and green for background) in 1¾ oz (50 gr) skeins.

For sweater only, 2 (2, 3, 3) skeins MC and 1 skein or ½ oz (14 gr) of each CC.

For hat only, 1 skein MC and 1 skein or ¼ oz (7 gr) of each CC.

For socks only, 1 skein MC and 1 skein or ¼ oz (7 gr) of each CC.

For entire set, 2 (2, 3, 3) skeins MC and 1 skein or 1 oz (28 gr) of each CC.

Knitting needles sizes 2 and 1, one pair of each (or one pair of the size that gives you the correct gauge, and one pair a size smaller).

DP needles in the above sizes, one set of 5 in the larger size, and one set of 4 in the smaller size.

2 st holders.
9 st markers.
A tapestry needle.
2 ⅜" buttons (we used mother-of-pearl buttons).

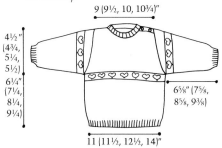

Correct gauge is important

7 sts = 1", 11 rows = 1" in St st. To ensure the correct finished measurements, take time to check gauge. Make a sample swatch: with the larger size needles, cast on 28 sts. Work 44 rows in St st. Lay swatch flat and measure it—without bunching or stretching, swatch should be 4" square. If swatch is too small, try again with larger needles; if it is too large, try smaller needles.

SWEATER

The back

With smaller needles and MC, cast on 80 (82, 86, 98) sts, and work in k 1, p 1 ribbing for ⅝". Change to larger needles. Work in St st until the back measures 4⅞ (5⅞, 6⅞, 7⅞)" from beg, end on wrong side of work, ready for a k row. Cut MC.

♥ Panel for sweater
The first 3 rows are written out. See how they correspond to the ♥ Chart for Body as you work them, then follow the chart for the remainder of the ♥ Panel.

96

Note: Stranding is the technique of working with more than one color across a row, as in the ♥ Panel of our knitted set. Carry yarns at even tension across the wrong side of work, overlapping them by bringing the strand of color in current use under or over the strand of color previously used. The photo detail of wrong side of ♥ Panel shows the yarns overlapped at every st, but you can overlap every 2nd or every 3rd st if you prefer.

Join background color (we used green for background, red for ♥)

Row 1: K.

Row 2: P.

Row 3: K 10 (11, 8, 9) green, k 1 red, *k 9 green, k 1 red, rep from * to last 9 (10, 7, 8) sts, end k 9 (10, 7, 8) green.

Row 4-10: Follow ♥ Chart for Body, rows 4 through 10. Cut green and red strands. This completes the ♥ panel.

Join MC and continue in St st until Back measures 6¼ (7¼, 8¼, 9¼)" from beg, or desired length to armhole.

Shape the back armholes

Row 1 and 2: Bind off 3 (3, 3, 4) sts at beg of each row—74 (76, 80, 90 sts.

Row 3 and 4: Bind off 2 (2, 2, 3) sts at beg of each row—70 (72, 76, 84) sts.

Row 5 and 6: Bind off 2 (2, 2, 2) sts at beg of each row—66 (68, 72, 80) sts.

Row 7-10: Bind off 1 (1, 1, 1,) st at beg of each row—62 (64, 68, 76) sts.

Work even until armhole measures 4 (4¼, 4¾, 5¼)" deep.

Knitting

Shape the back neck

K the first 26 (27, 28, 32) sts of next row, bind off the next 10 (10, 12, 12) sts for center back neck edge, place the first 26 (27, 28, 32) sts on st holder, k the rem 26 (27, 28, 32) sts. P 1 row.

Shape the left back neck edge: Bind off the first 10 (10, 10, 12) sts of next row, k to end—16 (17, 18, 20) sts. Work even until left armhole measures 4½ (4¾, 5¼, 5½)" deep.

Make the button placket: Work the next 6 rows in k 1, p 1 ribbing. Bind off in ribbing.

Shape the right back neck edge: With right side of work facing you, sl the sts from st holder onto needle, join MC; k across. Bind off the first 10 (10, 10, 12) sts of next row to mirror the left neck edge. Work even on 16 (17, 18, 20) sts until right armhole measures same as left armhole, minus the ribbing. Bind off.

The front

Work in the same manner as the back, including the ♥   l, until the armhole measures 2½ (2¾, 3, 3½)" deep.

Divide work

K the first 26 (27, 28, 32) sts of next row, bind off the next 10 (10, 12, 12) sts for center front neck edge, place the first 26 (27, 28, 32) sts on st holder, k the rem 26 (27, 28, 32) sts. P 1 row.

Shape the left front neck edge:

Row 1: Bind off 3 (3, 3, 3) sts at beg of row, k to end—23 (24, 25, 29) sts.

Row 2-12: P.

Row 3: Bind off 2 (2, 2, 3) sts at beg of row, k to end—21 (22, 23, 26) sts.

Row 5: Bind off 2 (2, 2, 3) sts at beg of row, k to end—19 (20, 21, 23) sts.

Row 7-11: Bind off 1 st at beg of each row, k to end—16 (17, 18, 20) sts.

Work even until left armhole measures same as back armhole. Bind off.

Shape the right front neck edge

Sl the sts from st holder onto needle and reverse the above shaping so that the right neck edge mirrors the left. Work even until right armhole measures same as left armhole, end on right side of work, ready for a p row.

This close-up of the right side of the ♥ panel demonstrates that fine, even stranding on the wrong side keeps holes or puckers from turning up on the right side.

This is the wrong side of the ♥ panel. It shows the unusually careful stranding technique. Note that the yarns are twisted at every stitch, rather than every second or third stitch, which is more common. Stranding every stitch, if done correctly, will make the work lie flat and the wrong side look neat, and feel smoother on the side that comes into direct contact with the infant's skin. See ♥ panel and stranding instructions.

This is a detail of the button placket fastening on the left shoulder of sweater. It also shows the neck ribbing, part of which is picked up along the placket edge. The second buttonhole is worked in the neck ribbing. The buttons are ⅜" mother-of-pearl. See Back, Shape the neck, and Front, Shape the neck.

Make the buttonhole placket
Row 1 and 2: K 1, p 1 rib.
Row 3: Rib first 8 (8, 9, 10) sts, bind off next 2 sts for buttonhole, rib rem sts.
Row 4: Rib first 6 (7, 7, 8) sts, cast on 2 sts over bound-off sts, rib rem sts.
Row 5 and 6: K 1, p 1 rib.
Bind off in ribbing.

The sleeve

With smaller needles and MC, cast on 44 (46, 50, 52) sts and work k 1, p 1 ribbing for ⅝". Change to larger needles and St st, inc 8 (10, 8, 10) sts evenly spaced across the first St st row—52 (56, 58, 62) sts.
Note: The ♥ panel begins on the 53rd row after the ribbing. For the 12 month, 18 month, and 24 month sizes, the ♥ panel will begin before the sleeve increases (see below) are finished. As you work the sleeve inc, keep track of the number of rows you work and the number of sts on the needle so that you begin the ♥ panel in the right place.

Inc at each end every 6th row 6 (4, 8, 11) times, then every 8th row 2 (5, 3, 2) times. When you have completed 52 rows, there should be 68 (70, 74, 78) sts on the needle, and your work should measure 5⅜" from beg.

♥ Panel for sleeve
Beg with a k row, work the sleeve ♥ panel, following the ♥ chart for sleeves. Then continue with MC and any rem inc until sleeve measures 6⅝ (7⅝, 8⅝, 9⅜)" from beg or desired length to under-arm—68 (74, 80, 88) sts.

Shape the sleeve cap
Row 1-4: Bind off 4 (5, 5, 5) sts at beg of each row—52 (54, 60, 68) sts.
Row 5-8: Bind off 5 (5, 5, 5) sts at beg of each row—32 (34, 40, 48) sts.
Row 9, 10: Bind off 5 (5, 6, 5) sts at beg of each row—22 (24, 28, 38) sts.
Row 11, 12: Bind off 5 (6, 6, 5) sts at beg of each row—12 (12, 16, 28) sts.
Row 13, 14: 24 month size only: Bind off 6 sts at beg of each row—16 sts.
All sizes: Bind off rem 12 (12, 16, 16) sts. Make 2 sleeves.

CHART FOR SWEATER BODY

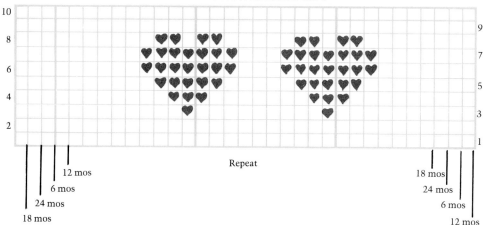

Follow chart from the bottom line to the top line. Begin and end at the points designated for the size you are making, and repeat the center section. Follow chart lines alternately from left to right on knit rows (odd-numbered), and from right to left on purl rows (even-numbered).

CHART FOR SLEEVE

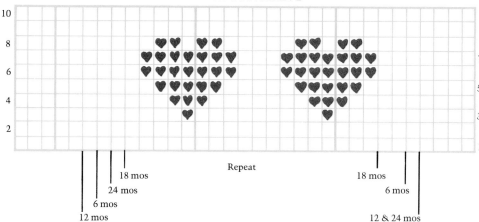

Follow chart from the top line to the bottom line. Begin and end at the points designated for the size you are making, and repeat the center section. Follow chart lines alternately from left to right on knit rows (odd-numbered), and from right to left on purl rows (even-numbered).

Finishing the garment

With tapestry needle and yarn, sew right shoulder seam.
Neck border: Work back and forth in rows. We used dp needles for their flexibility around corners. You can use a standard needle if you work more comfortably with it. With smaller size dp needles, and with right side of work facing you, pick up 83 (83, 91, 91) sts around neck opening.
Row 1 and 2: K 1, p 1 rib.

Row 3: Rib to last 5 sts, bind off next 2 sts for buttonhole, rib rem sts.
Row 4: K 1, p 1 rib, casting on 2 sts over the bound-off sts.
Row 5 and 6: K 1, p 1 rib across each row. Bind off loosely in ribbing.

Pin left shoulder so that front overlaps back. Sew side and sleeve seams. Set in sleeves. Sew on buttons. Weave in ends of yarn. Overcast buttonhole edges if desired.

LONG SOCKS

CHART FOR SOCK

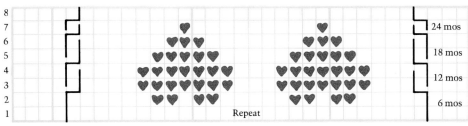

Repeat

24 mos
18 mos
12 mos
6 mos

Follow chart from the bottom line to the top line. Begin and end at the points designated for the size you are making, and repeat the center section. Follow every line of chart from left to right, and knit every round. ♥ chart for sock is two lines shorter than ♥ charts for sweater.

Finished sock circumference: 6½ (7, 7½, 8)". Use the same yarn as you used for the sweater. You will also need dp needles, both sets, and 2 st markers for the socks. *Note:* To prevent stretched sts where the dp needles cross, the first st on each needle must be worked very tightly.

With MC and one smaller size dp needle, cast on 46 (50, 54, 58) sts. Being careful not to twist sts, in k 1, p 1 ribbing work the first 16 (16, 18, 20) sts onto a 2nd dp needle, the next 15 (17, 18, 19) sts onto a 3rd needle, and the last 15 (17, 18, 19) sts onto a 4th needle. Do not turn; join and continue in rnds of k 1, p 1 ribbing for ¾". Change to larger needles and St st.
Next rnd: K 7 (7, 8, 9), place marker on needle, k 2, place marker on needle (the 2 sts now inside markers are the center back of sock), k rem 7 (7, 8, 9) sts from first needle. K rem sts of rnd.

Continue in St st (k every rnd) for 2 more rnds, then k the first 8 (8, 9, 10) sts of first needle (you should have worked 1 st inside markers). Cut MC.

♥ **Panel for sock**
Join green, and follow ♥ chart for sock, dec outside markers on the 3rd (5th, 7th, 8th) rnd of ♥ panel by working k 2 tog after the 2nd marker, and SKP before the first marker.
Note: Because you are working in rnds, each line of ♥ chart must be followed from left to right. Because sock is knitted from the top down, ♥ chart begins at top of ♥. Sock ♥ panel is 2 lines narrower than sweater ♥ panel.

After the ♥ panel, cut CC's, join MC. Continuing in St st, rep the dec on the first (5th, 9th, 12th) rnd after ♥ panel, and every 6th (8th, 10th, 12th) rnd twice more—38 (42, 46, 50) sts. Work even until sock measures 4½ (4¾, 5¼, 5½)" from beg.

Shape the heel
K around until within 8 (9, 10, 11) sts of first marker. Divide sts onto 2 needles—18 (20, 22, 24) sts for heel on one needle (the sts inside markers, plus 8 (9, 10, 11 sts on either side of markers), and the rem 20 (22, 24, 26) sts for front of sock on the other needle. On the 18 (20, 22, 24) heel sts only, work 8 (10, 12, 14) rows even in St st (k 1 row, p 1 row).

Work short rows: k 17 (19, 21, 23), turn (leave 1 st unworked on left needle), p 16 (18, 20, 22), turn (leave 1 st unworked on left needle), k 15 (17, 19, 21), turn (2 sts unworked), p 14 (16, 18, 20), turn, k 13 (15, 17, 19), turn, p 12 (14, 16, 18), turn, k 11 (13, 15, 17), turn, p 10 (12, 14, 16), turn, k to end. P 1 row, k 1 row across all 18 (20, 22, 24) heel sts.
Divide for heel gusset shaping: Take a 3rd dp needle and pick up 8 (10, 12, 14) sts along the nearest edge of the 8 (10, 12, 14) rows worked even previous to the short rows. Take a 4th needle and k across the 20 (22, 24, 26) sts for front of sock. Take the free needle and pick up 8 (10, 12, 14) sts along the other edge of the 8 (10, 12, 14) rows worked even. Transfer 1 st from each end of the heel sts onto each side needle. The sock is now divided onto 4 needles—16 (18, 20, 22) sts for heel, 9 (11, 13, 15) sts at each side, and

20 (22, 24, 26) sts for front—(54 (62, 70, 78) sts. Take care to maintain these 4 sets of sts throughout the foll dec rnds.
Dec rnd: K 16 (18, 20, 22) heel sts of first needle, k to within last 2 sts of 2nd needle, k 2 tog, k 20 (22, 24, 26) sts of 3rd needle, SKP, k rem sts of 4th needle.

Rep dec rnd every other rnd 7 (9, 11, 13) times more, until there is 1 st left on each side needle—38 (42, 46, 50) sts.

Sock foot
Distribute the 38 (42, 46, 50) sts evenly onto 3 needles. Work even in rnds until foot measures 1¾ (2, 2¼, 2¾)" or desired length to toe. Cut MC.

Shape the toe
Join green. Dec every other rnd 8 (10, 12, 14) times by SKP before first marker and k 2 tog after 2nd marker—22 sts. Bind off. Sew up toe, and weave in the ends of yarn.

This detail of the foot of the sock shows both the heel gusset and the toe shaping. The gusset stitches are picked up along each edge of the heel. The front stitches are joined to the heel and gusset stitches. The gusset stitches are decreased to obtain the stitches for the foot and toe shaping.

HAT

♥ Panel for hat
Join green, and follow ♥ chart for hat. Note that the ♥ panel for hat is 2 rows narrower than ♥ panel for sweater, and starts on a p row.

Shape the crown
Join MC and work even in St st until hat measures 3¼ (3¾, 4, 4¼)" from beg, or desired depth to crown, end on wrong side of work, ready for a k row. Dec across next row as foll: k 1, *place marker on needle, k 2 tog, k 12 (13, 13, 14), rep from * 8 times more, end k 1—119 (128, 128, 137) sts.
Rep dec every k row by k 2 tog after each marker 6 (7, 7, 8) times more—65 sts. P 1 row.
Next row: K 1, *k 2 tog, rep from * across row—33 sts.

Looking at the hat from the top shows the alignment of decreases and the pleated effect created by gathering the stitches of the last round. See HAT, Shape the crown.

Rep last 2 rows once—17 sts. Cut yarn, leaving enough to thread through rem sts and sew back seam. Sew seam. Weave in the ends of yarn.

Finished hat circumference: 18 (19½, 19½, 21)". Use the same yarn and needles as you used for the sweater. You will also need 9 st markers for the hat.

With MC and smaller needles, cast on 128 (137, 137, 146) sts. Work in k 1, p 1 ribbing for ¾". P 1 row. Change to larger needles and work in St st until piece measures 2 (2½, 2¾, 3)" from beg, end on right side of work, ready for a p row. Cut MC.

CHART FOR HAT

Repeat

24 mos

12 & 18 mos

6 mos

All sizes

Follow chart from the bottom line to the top line. Begin and end at the points designated for the size you are making, and repeat the center section. Follow chart lines alternately from left to right on knit rows (odd-numbered), and from right to left on purl rows (even-numbered). ♥ chart for hat is two lines shorter than ♥ charts for sweater.

Rompin' Overalls

These roomy, action overalls are of ingenious construction as well as flexible fit. They are knitted flat in one piece, and at first glance they look seamless. All edgings and details are knitted in—there are no stitches to pick up. The major seams are sewn along the inside legs and up the back. The overalls are made of sport weight wool, mostly in stockinette stitch, with a pebbly pattern stitch on the contrasting color bib. Their shape is like a baby's shape—plump and cheerful. We used heathery gray and soft pink (medium value colors are slower to show dirt).

The generous fit around tummy and legs permits ease of movement and provides plenty of room for diapers and other layers of clothing, and of course, growth.

In colder weather, the overalls could go over thermal underwear and a blouse, and be topped by a sweater. Please remember that layering is most effective with lightweight garments that allow freedom of movement and are made of natural fibers or natural fiber blends. Layers trap insulating air between them, and natural fibers let perspiration evaporate through them rather than stay trapped inside and turn clammy.

Rompin' overalls instructions are given for 6 months size, with changes for 12 months, 18 months, and 24 months sizes in parentheses. Overalls are for 22 (24, 26, 28)" chest sizes and measure 26 (29, 31, 35)" around tummy section.

Shop for these items

Sport weight yarn in 1¾ oz. (50 gr) skeins, 3 (3, 4, 4) skeins MC (we used gray), 1 (1, 1, 1) skein CC (we used pink).

Knitting needles size 4 and size 2, or 1 pair to knit the indicated gauge, plus 1 pair 2 sizes smaller.

2 large st holders

2 small st holders or safety pins

2⅝" buttons (we used buttons to match the CC yarn).

Correct gauge is important

6 sts = 1", 8 rows = 1" in St st. To ensure the correct finished measurements, take time to check gauge. Make a sample swatch: with the larger size needles, cast on 24 sts. Work in St st for 32 rows. Lay swatch flat and measure it. Without bunching or stretching, swatch should measure 4 x 4" square. If swatch is too big, try again with smaller needles, if it is too small, try larger needles.

Rompin' leg

With smaller size needles and CC, cast on 52 (57, 61, 66) sts. Work in k 1, p 1, ribbing for 2 rows, cut CC. Join MC and continue until ribbing measures 3¼" from beg, drop MC, join CC, work 2 more rib rows, cut CC.

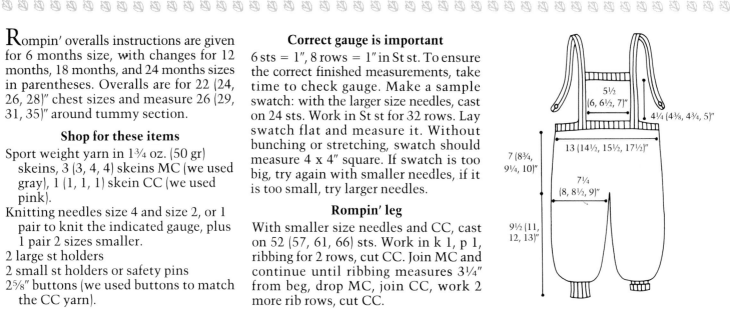

5½ (6, 6½, 7)"

4¼ (4⅜, 4¾, 5)"

13 (14½, 15½, 17½)"

7 (8¾, 9¼, 10)"

7¼ (8, 8½, 9)"

9½ (11, 12, 13)"

Change to larger needles. Pick up MC and k 1 row, inc 35 (49, 41, 42) sts evenly spaced across—87 (96, 102, 108) sts. Work even until leg measures 9½(11, 12, 13)" from beg.

Shape crotch
Bind off 2 sts at beg of next 6 rows—75 (84, 90, 96) sts. Place rem sts on holder. Make 2 legs.

Tummy section

With right side of work facing, sl sts from holders onto one needle—150 (168, 180, 192) sts. With MC and larger size needles, work even until tummy section measures 7 (8¾, 9¼, 10)" from crotch shaping, dec 18 (24, 24, 24) sts evenly spaced across last row—132 (144, 156, 168) sts. Change to smaller needles and work k 1, p 1 ribbing for ¼", end ready for a right side row.

Make buttonholes
Row 1: Rib first 22 (24, 26, 28) sts, bind off next 2 sts, rib to last 24 (26, 28, 30) sts, bind off next 2 sts, rib rem sts.
Row 2: Work across, cast on 2 sts over each pair of bound-off sts.
Work 2 rows even in ribbing.

Wrong side view of intersecting crotch seams. The horizontal seam runs along the inside leg from ankle to ankle. The vertical seam joins the front and back crotch shapings and continues up the overalls back.

Rompin' bib

Bind off loosely in ribbing 44 (48, 52, 56) sts at beg of next 2 rows—44 (48, 52, 56) center sts rem. Cut MC. Sl 6 sts from each end of row to safety pins or small holders—32 (36, 40, 44) sts.

Begin pattern stitch
With right side facing, larger size needles, and CC, work across in established k1, p1 r.b.
Row 1 (wrong side): P.
Row 2: * P 1, k 2, rep from * across.
Row 3: P.
Row 4: * K 1, p 1, rep from * across.
Rep rows 1-4 until bib measures 4¼ (4⅜, 4¾, 5)", end ready for a right side row. Cut CC. With right side facing, smaller size needles, and MC, k across all sts.

This is the right side of the bib. The ribbing at the top of the tummy section is bound off at the back and sides. The front stitches are divided into three separately worked groups. A large center group knits into the contrasting color bib, topped with a few more rows of ribbing in the main color. Six stitches on either side of the bib are knitted with the main color into long ribbed strips which border the sides of the bib and then extend past it to form the straps.

Work 4 rows in k 1, p 1 ribbing. Bind off loosely in ribbing.

Rompin' straps

With smaller size needles and MC, work the 6 sts from each bib holder in k 1, p 1 ribbing as established for 15¾ (17¼, 18, 18¾)". Bind off loosely in ribbing.

Rompin' finishing

With tapestry needle and yarn, sew back seam and crotch seam. Sew inner leg seams, reversing seam on lower half of ankle ribbing. Sew strap edges to either side of bib, extending straps 11 (12⅛, 13¼, 13¾)" past top edge of bib. Sew one button to free end of each strap. Turn up ankle ribbing to form cuffs.

Zippered Turtleneck Pullover

We choose to avoid the pretentiousness of calling this sweater "classic", yet it has many enduring virtues. In few words, it is both very plain and very simple. You knit it in flat pieces, almost entirely of stockinette stitch, with tapered raglan sleeves, straight body, zippered turtleneck, and ribbed front placket. Like the "little black dress" in your wardrobe and the flour in your pantry, it is a staple.

A solid color turtleneck with an easy-access zipper is also very practical. Raglan and straight seamlines are the easiest to sew, and there are no stitches to pick up at the neckline—they are all knitted right off the holders. This sweater is good news for the knitter who wishes to make a useful, lasting contribution to a child's wardrobe, but is in a hurry or just doesn't crave a challenge this time around.

If you do crave a challenge, and you like the shape of this sweater, here are some variations. Use sport weight yarn instead of fingering weight, and knit extra tightly or on smaller needles to get the gauge, for a denser, thicker, warmer fabric; or substitute a favorite pattern stitch for the stockinette stitch, again being careful of gauge; or use your odds and ends of yarn to knit stripes in or embroider designs on.

Adjust the turtleneck depth as you like, and install a zipper of corresponding length (a little extra zipper length can be hidden by allowing the surplus to extend below the opening on the wrong side). Omit the zipper entirely, or split the front all the way down for a zippered cardigan.

Pullover instructions are written for a 6 months size, followed by larger sizes in parentheses: (12 months, 18 months, 24 months). The finished chest measurements are 21 (23, 25, 27)".

Shop for these items

Baby yarn, fingering yarn, or sport weight yarn to knit the indicated gauge; 3 (3, 4, 4) 1¾ oz (50 gr) skeins.
Knitting needles sizes 3 and 1, one pair of each (or one pair of the size that gives you the correct gauge, and one pair 2 sizes smaller. If you use sport weight yarn, you may need smaller sizes to get the gauge).
1 16" circ or set of dp needles in the smaller size.
1 short zipper to match or complement the yarn color.
Matching cotton sewing thread.
5 st holders.
1 tapestry needle.

Correct gauge is important

7 sts = 1", 10 rows = 1", in St st. To ensure the correct finished measurements, take time to check gauge. Make a sample swatch: with the larger size needles, cast on 28 sts. Work 40 rows in St st. Lay swatch flat and measure it—without bunching or stretching, swatch should be 4" square. If swatch is too small, try again with larger needles; if it is too large, try smaller needles.

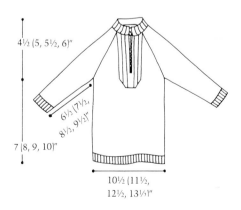

4½ (5, 5½, 6)"

6½ (7½, 8½, 9½)"

7 (8, 9, 10)"

10½ (11½, 12½, 13½)"

The back

With smaller needles, cast on 76 (84, 92, 100) sts. Work in k 2, p 2 rib for 1½", inc 1 (1, 1, 0) st at each end of last rib row—78 (86, 94, 100) sts. Change to larger needles and St st. Work even until back measures 7 (8, 9, 10)" from beg or desired length to underarm, ending on right side of work, ready for a p row.

Shape the back raglan armholes
Dec row: SKP, k across to last 2 sts, k 2 tog.
Next row: P.
Rep these 2 rows 21 (24, 27, 29) times more, until there are 34 (36, 38, 40) sts on needle. Back armhole should measure app 4½ (5, 5½, 6)". Place rem sts on holder.

The front

Work in the same manner as the back until front measures 1" less than back to underarm, or to the point where you want the zipper opening to begin, less 1", end on wrong side of work, ready for a k row. (If you want to place the zipper lower, you will have to divide the work for the zipper opening before you begin the armhole shaping.)

Zipper placket
Row 1: K 36 (40, 44, 47), p 2, k 2, p 2, k 36 (40, 44, 47).
Row 2: P 36 (40, 44, 47), k 2, p 2, k 2, p 36 (40, 44, 47).
Row 3 and 4: Rep Row 1 and 2.
Row 5: K 32 (36, 40, 43), p 2, * k 2, p 2, rep from * twice more, end k 32 (36, 40, 43).
Row 6: P 32 (36, 40, 43), k 2, * p 2, k 2, rep from * twice more, end p 32 (36, 40, 43).
Shape the front armholes
Row 7: SKP, k 30 (34, 38, 41), p 2, * k 2, p 2, rep from * twice more, end k 30 (34, 38, 41), k 2 tog—76 (84, 92, 98) sts.
Row 8: P 31 (35, 39, 42), k 2, *p 2, k 2, rep from * twice more, end p 31 (35, 39, 42).

Divide the front for neck opening
Row 9: SKP, k 25 (29, 33, 36), p 2, * k 2, p 2, rep from * once more, k 3 tog, p 2, p 2 twice, k 25 (29, 33, 36), end k 2 tog—72 (80, 88, 94) sts.

Row 10: P 26 (30, 34, 37), * k 2, p 2, rep from * once more, k 1, p 1, drop yarn, join a 2nd ball of yarn to rem sts of row, p 1, k 1, * p 2, k 2, rep from * once more, p 26 (30, 34, 37)—36 (40, 44, 47) sts each side.

Row 11: SKP, k 24 (28, 32, 35), * p 2, k 2, rep from * once more, p 1, k 1, pick up yarn from other side of neck, k 1, p 1, * k 2, p 2, rep from * once more, k 24 (28,

The lower end of the placket ribbing on the front of the sweater is curved by beginning the ribbing on 6 center sts and gradually widening to 14 sts. The ribbing is worked for 1½". The front is then divided in half. The work is continued in two sections to form the opening for the zipper.

This is the top center section of the pullover, seen from the right side. The turtleneck is folded to the outside and the edge stitched down. The zipper reaches to the folded edge. The raglan seams are both functional and decorative.

32, 35), end k 2 tog—35 (39, 43, 46) sts each side.
Row 12: K the k sts and p the p sts across both sides of neck.

Working across both sides of front neck each row, continue dec every right side row by SKP at beg of row and k 2 tog at end of row, and work all wrong side rows same as row 12, until 16 (17, 18, 19) sts rem on each side of front neck opening. Neck opening will be app 4" deep. Sl rem sts to st holders.

The sleeve

With smaller needles, cast on 36 (40, 44, 48) sts. Work in k 2, p 2 ribbing for 1½", inc 4 sts evenly spaced across last rib row—40 (44, 48, 52) sts. Change to larger needles and St st, inc 1 st at each end of first row above rib, rep inc every 5th row 5 (6, 7, 8) times more—52, (58, 64, 70) sts. Work even until sleeve measures 6½ (7½, 8½, 9½)" from beg or desired length to underarm, ending on right side of work, ready for a p row.

Shape the sleeve cap
Dec row: SKP, k across to last 2 sts, k 2 tog.
Next row: P.
Rep these 2 rows 21 (24, 27, 29) times more, until there are 8 (8, 8, 10) sts left on needle. Sl rem sts to st holder. Make 2 sleeves.

Finishing the garment

With tapestry needle and yarn, sew raglan seams. Sew side and sleeve seams. Weave in the ends of yarn. Turtleneck: Sl all sts on holders to circ or dp needles. Join yarn and work in k 2, p 2 ribbing for 1½" or to desired depth. Bind off loosely in ribbing. Fold turtleneck over to right side and sew bound-off edge to sweater, keeping stitches elastic. Sew both thicknesses of turtleneck together along front zipper opening. Baste zipper in place. With right side of sweater facing and matching sewing thread, overcast the edge of the neck opening to the zipper fabric by hand, or machine stitch close to edge, being careful not to stretch the knitting.

Heavy
Weather
Set

*Knitted Sweater,
Hat, and Mittens*

he deep raglan armholes of our heavy weather pullover allow for plenty of heavy weather movements—like packing and throwing snowballs while it is still snowing, pulling sleds, and making snow angels—or just keeping warm and dry while watching mom and dad show how all those wintertime classic movements are done. Knitted in soft sport weight wool, the sweater, hat, and mittens will keep a child warm.

The knitted part of this outfit employs two useful methods of changing colors—color block knitting and stranding—to make the contrasting-color rope cables. These cables run down the center of the sweater front, back, and sleeves and the back of each mitten. A group of cables converges at the top of the hat. If you've never tried color block knitting or stranding, take the opportunity to learn them now. Familiarity with these techniques can add new texture to your future knitting.

Make this outfit in a roomy size and it will be wearable for a longer time. While it is a little too big, you can roll up the sleeves and layer other clothing under it for extra warmth.

Heavy weather set instructions are given for 6 month size, with changes for 12 months, 18 months, and 24 months sizes in parentheses. Finished chest measurements are 22 (24, 26, 28)".

Shop for these items
Sport weight yarn, 3 1¾ oz (50 gr) skeins MC (we used dark blue), and 1 skein CC (we used white).
Knitting needles size 4 and 2, or size to knit the indicated gauge, plus 1 pair 2 sizes smaller.
DP needles in the above sizes.
1 cable needle.

2 stitch markers.
4 stitch holders.
1 tapestry needle.

Correct gauge is important
6 sts = 1", 8 rows = 1", in St st. To ensure the correct finished measurements, take time to check gauge. Make a sample swatch: with the larger size needles, cast on 24 sts. Work 32 rows in St st. Lay swatch flat and measure it. Without bunching or stretching, swatch should be 4" square. If swatch is too small, try again with larger needles; if it is too large, try smaller needles.

Knitting

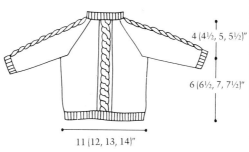

SWEATER

The back

With smaller needles and MC, cast on 68 (74, 80, 86) sts. Work in k 1, p 1 ribbing for 1½". Change to larger needles.
Note: The contrasting-color center cable is produced by working with three balls of yarn above the ribbing. When changing from one color to the next, the yarns must be twisted around each other to prevent holes or bumps in the fabric.

If you wish to make the back plain, with no cable, work even with MC in St st until ready to shape armholes.

Begin cable pattern
Row 1: With MC, k 26 (29, 32, 35), p 2, drop MC, join CC, k 12, drop CC, join 2nd ball of MC, p 2, k 26 (29, 32, 35).
Row 2: With MC, p 26 (29, 32, 35), k 2, with CC, p 12, with MC, k2, p 26 (29, 32, 35).
Row 3: With MC, p 26 (29, 32, 35), k 2, with CC, sl next 6 sts to CN and hold at front of work, k 6, k 6 from CN, with MC, p 2, k 26 (29, 32, 35).
Row 4-8: K the k and p the p sts, changing yarns as established.
Rep rows 1-8 until piece measures 6 (6½, 7, 7½)" from beg, end ready for a right side row.

Note: Maintain cable pattern and color changes as established throughout shaping.

Shape armholes
Bind off 6 sts at beg of next 2 rows—56 (62, 68, 74) sts. Dec one st each end of next row and every other row a total of 15 (17, 19, 21) times—26 (28, 30, 32) sts. Armhole should measure about 4 (4½, 5, 5½)" deep. Sl rem sts to st holder for back of neck.

Please refer to page 111 for diagrams of "color block" knitting technique.

The front

Work the front in the same manner as the back.

The sleeve

With smaller needles and MC, cast on 38 (40, 43, 44) sts. Work in k 1, p 1 ribbing for 1½". Charge to larger needles.
Begin cable pattern
Row 1: With MC, k 13 (14, 15, 16), p 2, with CC, k 8, with 2nd ball of MC, p 2, k 13 (14, 15, 16).
Row 2: With MC, p 13 (14, 15, 16), k 2, with CC, p 8, with MC, p 13 (14, 15, 16).
Row 3: With MC, k 1, inc in next st, k 11 (12, 13, 14), p 2, with CC, sl next 4 sts to CN and hold in front of work, k 4, k 4 from CN, with MC, p 2, k 11 (12, 13, 14), inc in next st, k 1—2 sts added.
Row 4-8: K the k and p the p sts, inc at each end of 8th row—2 sts added.

Rep rows 1-8 until these are 50 (54, 58, 62) sts on needle. Work even until sleeve measures 6½ (7½, 8½, 9½)" from beg or desired length to underarm, end ready for a right side row.

Shape sleeve cap
Maintaining center cable pattern, shape sleeve cap in exactly the same manner as the back and front armholes—8 (8, 8, 8) sts. Cap should measure about 4 (4½, 5, 5½)" or same as armhole. Sl rem sts to st holder. Make 2 sleeves.

Looking closely at the upper portion of the finished sweater, you can see the neat joining of the raglan seams, and the color block knitting technique used for the center cables. Each color area has its own ball of yarn. When changing from one yarn to the next, the strands are twisted around one another. The twist should not be visible on the right side of the work.

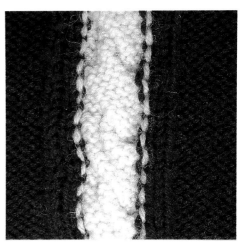

Another view of the center cable on the finished sweater, wrong side out. The twisting of the yarns in color block knitting appears in a vertical ridge on the wrong side of the work.

Finishing the sweater

With tapestry needle and yarn, sew raglan seams, side and sleeve seams. With right side of work facing, smaller size dp needles, and MC, k sts off all holders and distribute evenly on 3 needles. Work in rnds of k 1, p 1 ribbing for 3" or to desired turtleneck depth. Bind off loosely in ribbing. Weave in the ends of yarn.

Diagram measurements: 4 (4½, 5, 5½)" ; 6 (6½, 7, 7½)" ; 11 (12, 13, 14)"

MITTENS

Note: The 6 month size mittens are made without thumbs.

Right mitten

With smaller size needles and MC cast on 41 (41, 41, 45) sts. Work in k 1, p 1 ribbing for 1¾ (1¾, 1¾, 2¼)", dec 4 (3, 3, 3) sts evenly spaced across last rib row—37 (38, 38, 42) sts. Change to larger size needles.

Hand. 6 Months Size Only

Row 1: With MC, k 3, p 2, join CC, k 8, join 2nd ball of MC, p 2, k 19.

Row 2: K the k and p the p sts, changing colors as established.

Row 3: With MC, k 3, p 2, with CC, slip next 4 sts to CN and hold in front of work, k 4, k 4 from CN, with MC, p 2, k rem sts.

Row 4-8: Rep row 2.

Rep rows 1-8 until mitten measures 5" from beg or ¾" less than desired length, end ready for a right side row.

Hand. 12, 18, and 24 Months Sizes

Row 1: With MC, k (3, 3, 4), p 2, join CC, k 8, join 2nd ball of MC, p 2 (3, 3, 4), place marker on needle, k (2, 2, 2), place marker on needle, k (18, 18, 20).

Row 2: K the k and p the p sts, slipping markers and changing colors as established.

Row 3: With MC, k (3, 3, 4), p 2, with CC, sl next 4 sts to CN and hold in front, k 4, k 4 from CN, p 2, k (3, 3, 4), inc in each of next 2 sts inside markers, k to end—(40, 40, 44) sts.

Row 4: Rep row 2.

Row 5: K the k and p the p sts, inc in st after first and before 2nd marker—(42, 42, 46) sts.

Row 6—8: Rep row 2.

Row 9: Rep row 5.

Row 10: Rep row 2.

For 24 months size only, rep row 3 once more, then work 3 rows even. Drop markers—(44, 44, 50) sts.

Thumb. 12, 18, and 24 Months sizes

Dividing row: Work established pat over first (17, 17, 19) sts of next row, sl these sts to st holder for back of hand, k (11, 11, 13) sts for thumb, sl rem (18, 18, 20) sts to 2nd st holder for palm, cast on 2

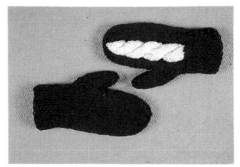

Mittens for the 12, 18, and 24 months sizes have thumbs. 2 stitches of the hand are increased gradually to form a gusset for the base of the thumb. The part of the thumb that emerges from the hand is then worked separately from the hand stitches.

sts for thumb, place marker on needle for beg of thumb—(13, 13, 15) sts on needle.

With MC, work even in St st until thumb is (½, ½, ¾)" deep, end ready for a k row.

Dec row 1: * k 1, k 2 tog, rep from * (3, 3, 4) times more, end k (1, 1, 0)—(9, 9, 10) sts.

Dec row 2: * k 2 tog, rep from * to last st, end k (1, 1, 0) – 5 sts.

Cut yarn, leaving a 9" end. Draw yarn through all sts twice, removing sts from needle. Draw sts tightly tog and fasten. Sew thumb seam.

Continue hand: Beg at edge of back hand, with right side facing, k (17, 17, 19) sts from holder to needle, join yarn, pick up 1 st in each of 2 cast-on thumb sts, k (18, 18, 20) sts from rem st holder—(37, 37, 41) sts. Continue in established cable pat until mitten hand measures (5, 5, 5½)" from beg or ¾" less than desired length, end ready for a right side row.

For All Sizes

Dec row 1: k 2, * k 2 tog, k 2, rep from * across, end k 1—28 (28, 28, 31) sts.

P 1 row.

Dec row 2: K 1, * k 2 tog, k 1, rep from * across—19 (19, 19, 21) sts.

P 1 row.

Dec row 3: * K 2 tog, rep from * across, end k 1—10 (10, 10, 11) sts.

Cut yarn, leaving a 9" end. Draw yarn through all sts twice, removing sts from needle. Draw sts tightly tog and fasten. Sew seam.

Left mitten

Work ribbing in same manner as for right mitten—37 (38, 38, 42) sts.

Hand. 6 Months Size Only

Row 1: k 19, place marker on needle, k 3, p 2, with CC, k 8, join 2nd half of MC, p 2, k 3.

Row 2: K the k and p the p sts, slipping marker and changing colors as established.

Row 3: With MC, k 22, p 2, with CC, sl next 4 sts to CN and hold in front, k 4, k 4 from CN, with MC, p 2, k 3.

Row 4-8: Rep row 2.

Rep rows 1-8 until mitten measures 5" from beg or ¾" less than desired length, end ready for a right side row.

Hand. 12, 18 and 24 Months Sizes Only

Row 1: With MC, k (18, 18, 20), place marker on needle, k (2, 2, 2), place marker on needle, k (3, 3, 4), p 2, with CC, k 8 join 2nd ball of MC, p 2, k (3, 3, 4).

Row 2: K the k and p the p sts, slipping markers and changing colors as established.

Row 3: With MC, k (18, 18, 20), sl marker, inc in each of next 2 sts, sl marker, k (3, 3, 4), p 2, with CC, sl next 4 sts to CN, k 4, k 4 sts from CN, with MC, p 2, k (3, 3, 4).

Row 4: Rep row 2.

Row 5: K the k and p the p sts, inc in st after first and before 2nd marker—(42, 42, 46) sts.

Row 6—8: Rep row 2.

Row 9: Rep row 5.

Row 10: Rep row 2.

For 24 months size only, rep row 3 once more, then work 3 rows even. Drop markets—(44, 44, 50) sts.

Thumb dividing row: Work established pattern over first (18, 18, 20) sts, sl these sts to holder for palm, k (11, 11, 13), sts for thumb, sl rem (17, 17, 19) sts to holder for back of hand, cast on 2 sts for thumb, place marker on needle for beg of thumb. Complete to mirror the right thumb.

Continue hand: Beg at edge of palm, with right side facing, k (18, 18, 20)) sts from holder pick up 1 st in each of 2 cast-on thumb sts, k sts from rem holder—(37, 37, 41) sts. Continue in established cable pattern until left mitten hand measures same as right mitten hand, end ready for a right side row.

For all sizes
Complete left mitten hand in same manner as right mitten hand.

HAT

Finished hat circumference: 18½ (18½, 21, 21)". With MC and 3 smaller size dp needles, cast on 112 (112, 128, 128) sts evenly distributed among the 3 needles, place marker for beg of rnds. Work in rnds of k 1, p 1 ribbing for 2½ (3, 3, 4)". Change to larger size dp needles. Work even in St st (k every rnd) until hat measures 4 (5, 5½, 6)" from beg.

Begin cable pattern

Note: The contrasting color cables on the hat are not worked with separate balls of yarn, like the sweater cables. They are made by carrying the yarns across the back of the work at even tension and overlapping them every 3rd or 4th stitch.

Rnd 1: k 8 MC, drop MC, join CC, k 8 CC, drop CC, rep from * around.
Rnd 2: Rep rnd 1.
Rnd 3: * K 8 MC, drop MC, sl next 4 sts to CN and hold in front of work, k 4 CC, k 4 CC from CN, drop CC, rep from * around.

Rnd 4: K around in established color pat, k 2 tog at beg of each MC section—7 (7, 8, 8) sts decreased.

Rnd 5 – 6: K around in established color pat.

Working a k 2 tog dec at beg of each MC section on every even rnd, rep rnds 1-6 until 1 st is left in each MC section—63 (63, 72, 72) sts. Cut MC. With CC, k 3 tog all around—21 (21, 24, 24) sts. K 2 tog all around—11 (11, 12, 12) sts. Cut yarn leaving a 6" end. Draw end of yarn through rem sts on needle, removing sts from needle. Draw sts tightly tog and fasten. Weave in the ends of yarn.

The hat is seen from the top with the right side out. It is knitted from corner edge to crown. The crown decreases are worked between the cables, causing them to converge.

This is the hat, also seen from the top, but with the wrong side out to show the stranding technique used to produce the contrasting-color cables. These cables are knitted on the sweater and mittens using the color block method, but on the hat the cables are so close together that stranding is more practical.

Knit side

Purl side

Color block knitting is the technique you use to make the contrasting-color cable up the center or the pullover and mittens. Each different colored area requires its own ball of yarn. When you work across a row, you change from one ball of yarn to the next, twisting the yarns around one another to join the "color blocks". On right side rows, bring the new color behind and over the old color; on wrong side rows, bring the new color in front of and over the old color. After working one stitch in the new color, pull firmly on the strand of the old color for a neat join between the sections, and drop the old color. If you do it correctly, at the join you will see an indentation on the right side of your knitting similar to the indentation between other stitches and a ridge on the wrong side that looks like a vertical row of garter stitch. The technique is the same whether you are changing from a stockinette stitch block to another stockinette stitch block as in our example, or from a stockinette block to a reverse stockinette block and vice versa, as in the Heavy Weather Set.

Lacy Cardigan and Bonnet

Knitted lace garments were very popular in 19th century Europe. Most were interpretations of costly bobbin-lace patterns. We used one of these time-honored lace stitches to beautify a child's cardigan and bonnet, edged with seed stitch and adorned with mother-of-pearl buttons. Decorative yarn-over raglan increases echo the lace panel. A length of pretty ribbon ties the bonnet.

The cardigan is made in one piece from the neck down, with all the pretty details knitted in. There is practically no "finishing" work to do, once you have bound off the last stitch—only two teeny-weeny baby sleeve seams to sew.

We chose seed stitch to border this set for several reasons. First of all, seed stitch performs well the function of a border—that of not allowing the fabric to curl. Second, it is a dressy stitch. Third, seed stitch lies perfectly flat—it neither expands or pulls in the edges of a garment. The sweater has, as a result, a clean, straight, elegant silhouette that adapts well to the young human form. After all, no two are exactly alike.

Instructions are given for 6 months size, with changes for 12 months, 18 months, and 24 months sizes in parentheses. The finished chest measurements are 21½ (23½, 25½, 27½)".

Shop for these items

Sport weight yarn—to make both pieces of the set, 3 1¾ oz (50 gr) skeins; to make bonnet only, 1 skein.

Knitting needles: size 4 or size to give gauge.

1 yard of ¼" wide ribbon.

6 ⅜" buttons.

6 stitch markers.

Correct gauge is important

6 sts = 1", 9 rows = 1" in St st. To ensure the correct finished measurements, take time to check gauge. Make a sample swatch: cast on 24 sts. Work 36 rows in St st. Lay swatch flat and measure it. Without bunching or stretching, swatch should be 4" square. If swatch is too small, try again with larger needles; if it is too large, try smaller needles.

Lace pattern stitch

This stitch is worked over 19 or 25 sts. *Note:* Each yo is counted and worked as one st.

Row 1 (right side): K 1, * yo, SKP, k 1, k 2 tog, yo, k 1, rep from * across.

Row 2: P.

Row 3: K 2, * yo, sl 1, k 2 tog, psso, yo, k 3, rep from * to last 5 sts, end yo, sl 1, k 2 tog, psso, yo, k 2.

Row 4: P.

Rep these 4 rows for lace pattern.

Yarn over

SWEATER

The yoke

Beg at neck edge, cast on 73 sts. Work 4 rows in seed st.

Begin lace panel

Work first 4 sts in seed stitch for right front border, k 23, place marker on needle for beg of lace panel, work row 1 of lace pattern over next 19 sts, place marker for end of lace panel, k 23, work rem 4 sts in seed st for left front border.

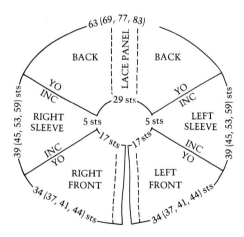

This diagram shows the shaping of the cardigan yoke. All sizes begin with the neck edging worked on 73 stitches. Two markers are placed on the needle for the lace panel, and four markers point out the raglan seams at indicated intervals. Increases are worked on both sides of the raglan markers until there is a total of 209 (233, 265, 289) stitches on the needle, distributed among back, fronts, and sleeves as shown.

Next row: Work 4 sts in seed st for border, p across to last 4 sts, slipping markers, work last 4 sts in seed st for border. Continue to work lace pat over center 19 sts, seed st over 4 border sts at each end, and St st over rem sts of foll rows, slipping markers every row.

Begin raglan increases

Work border sts, k 13, * yo, place marker on needle, inc in next st, k 3, inc in next st, place marker on needle, yo,* k 5, work row 3 of lace pat over next 19 sts, k 5, rep betw *'s once, end k 13, work border sts-81 sts.

On all foll right side rows of yoke, yo before and inc in st after each raglan marker, work lace panel betw lace panel markers, work border sts in seed st—8 sts added each row.

Buttonhole row

Always work buttonholes on wrong side rows, about 1¼" apart. The lowest buttonhole should come close to the lower edge of the sweater.

Girl's cardigan: (buttonholes on the right) Work first 2 (right border) sts, yo, k 2 tog, p across, work 4 (left border) sts.

Boy's cardigan: (buttonholes on the left) Work 4 (right border) sts, p across to left border, k 2 tog, yo, seed st over last 2 sts.

On all foll wrong side rows of yoke, work border sts in seed st, p all other sts, slipping markers. Continue to work lace panel, raglan inc, borders, buttonholes, and St st as established until there are 209 (233, 265, 289) sts on needle, ending ready for a wrong side row. Make a note of where you leave off with lace pat and buttonhole rows—you will be continuing them down the sweater body.

Divide work: Work first 34 (37, 41, 44) sts of next row, sl to st holder for right front, work next 39 (45, 53, 59) sts, sl to a 2nd st holder for right sleeve, work next 63 (69, 77, 83) sts, sl to a 3rd st holder for back, work next 39 (45, 53, 59) sts, sl to a 4th st holder for left sleeve, work rem 34 (37, 41, 44) sts, sl to a 5th st holder for left front.

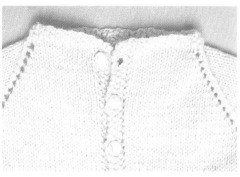

This view of the cardigan front shows some of the beautiful details that can be knitted right into a sweater. Like the lace panel, the raglan seams are worked with a diagonal yarn-over pattern. but each yarn-over is paired with an increase, adding two stitches to the work. Seed stitch is ideal for knitted-in borders because it has a fairly uniform appearance whether it is worked in a horizontal strip (e.g. the upper and lower borders) or a vertical strip (the front borders).

This is a close-up of the cardigan back, showing the back raglan increases, neck edging, and lace panel. This type of lace stitch, with yarn-overs and decreases forming delicate diagonal patterns, is called faggotting. The yarn-over puts an extra loop on the needle between two stitches, creating a hole in the work. The decrease which immediately precedes or succeeds the yarn-over compensates for the extra loop, and slants the pattern to the left or right.

The sleeve

With right side of work facing, sl the 39 (45, 53, 59) sts from one sleeve holder onto needle. Work even in St st until sleeve measures 6½ (7½, 8½, 9½)" from end of yoke, or ¾" short of desired length, dec 1 st each end of last row—37 (43, 51, 57) sts. Sleeve border: Work 7 rows in seed st. Bind off loosely in seed st. Work other sleeve in same manner.

The body

With right side of work facing, sl the 34 (37, 41, 44) sts of left front, the 63 (69, 77, 83) sts of back, and the 34 (37, 41, 44) sts of right front from their holders onto needle—131 (143, 159, 171) sts. You should be ready for a right side row.

Continuing with lace panel, borders, buttonholes, and St st as established, work even until body measures 7 (8, 9, 10)" from end of yoke, or ¾" short of desired length. Lower border: Work 7 rows in seed st. Bind off at even tension in seed st.

Finishing the garment

With tapestry needle and yarn, sew underarm seams. Sew buttons opposite buttonholes. Weave in the ends of yarn.

BONNET

Beg at front border, cast on 67 (73, 79, 85) sts. Work in seed st for 8 rows.

Begin lace panel
K 24 (27, 30, 30) sts, place marker on needle for beg of lace panel, work row 1 of lace pat over next 19 (19, 19, 25) sts, place marker on needle for end of lace panel, k rem 24 (27, 30, 30) sts. Continue to work lace panel over center 19 (19, 19, 25) sts and St st over 24 (27, 30, 30) sts on either side of lace panel, slipping markers every row, until bonnet measures 5 (6, 6½, 7)" from beg, end ready for a right side row.

Back of bonnet

Continuing lace and St st pat, bind off 21 (21, 24, 27) sts at beg of next 2 rows—25 (31, 31, 31) sts. Dec 1 st each end of next row—23 (29, 29, 29) sts. Rep dec every 4th row 1 (3, 3, 1) times more—21 (23, 23, 27) sts. Work even until bonnet back measures 3 (3, 3½, 4)", end ready for a right side row. Bind off at even tension.

Finishing the garment

With tapestry needle and yarn, sew edges of bonnet back to bound-off sts at either end of last long row. Eyelet border: With right side of work facing, pick up 72 (84, 90, 96) sts evenly spaced around lower edge of bonnet. Work in seed st for 2 rows. Make eyelets: Work 5 sts, * k 2 tog, yo, k 4, rep from * across, end last rep k 5.Work 2 rows in seed st. Bind off loosely in seed st. Weave in the ends of yarn. Weave ribbon through eyelets.

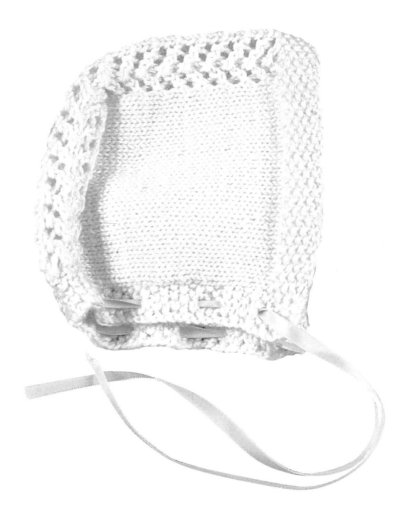

This is the bonnet, seen from the side. It is knitted flat, in a "T" shape. The bound-off stitches along the lower edge of the horizontal part of the "T" are sewn to the row edges of the vertical section, creating a three-dimensional curved shape that con-forms well to a baby's head. The lower border is picked up after sewing the seams. A row of eyelets is knitted into the border, and a pretty ribbon is threaded through the eyelets to make the bonnet tie.

Rocking Horse Pullover

Red is a highly symbolic color. It is prominent at bull fights and on sports cars. It is everpresent in the appetite-encouraging decor of restaurants. Old palaces are heavy with red upholstery and curtains.

There is no doubt about it—red is cheerful. It brightens even the palest complexion. If you don't know the sex of an unborn sweater recipient, red is one of the more interesting "compromise" colors. It also may make it easier, one day, for you to pick out your child in a huddle of baby blues and pinks, at nursery school or the day care center.

We have read that infant eyes respond most readily to bright colors, especially red, and even that a colorful environment aids the development of intelligence, or at least the ability to observe and distinguish differences.

We have taken a gloriously red yarn (because we like red too), and knitted it into a pert, short-sleeved pullover with a square peasant's neck. We have decorated the front of the sweater with two glossy embroidered rocking horses. The knitting is done with sport weight wool in stockinette stitch; the embroidery with cotton embroidery floss in cross stitch. Instructions are given for both puffed sleeves, as shown in our sample, and plain set-in sleeves, so that you can make the sweater for a boy or girl.

Pullover instructions are given for 6 months size, with changes for 12 months, 18 months, and 24 months sizes in parentheses. Finished chest measurements are 22 (24, 26, 28)".

Shop for these items

Sport weight yarn, 2 1¾ oz (50 gr) skeins MC (we used red), 1 skein CC (we used white).
Six-strand embroidery floss, 1 skein each blue and red or desired colors.
Knitting needles size 4 and 2, or one pair to knit the indicated gauge, and one pair two sizes smaller.
1 stitch holder.
1 tapestry needle.

Correct gauge is important

6 sts = 1", 8 rows = 1", working in St st. To ensure correct finished measurements, take time to check gauge. Make a sample swatch: with the larger size needles, cast on 24 sts. Work in St st for 32 rows. Lay swatch flat and measure it. Without bunching or stretching, swatch should be 4" square. If swatch is too big, try again with smaller needles; if it is too small, try larger needles.

The back

With smaller needles and MC, cast on 60 (66, 72, 78) sts. Work in k 1, p 1 ribbing for 1½", inc 6 sts evenly spaced across last rib row—66 (72, 78, 84) sts. Change

to larger needles and St st. Work even until back measures 6 (6½, 7, 7½)" from beg or desired lenghth to underarm, end on wrong side ready for a k row.

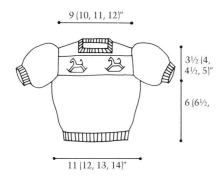

9 (10, 11, 12)"

3½ (4, 4½, 5)"

6 (6½,

11 (12, 13, 14)"

Shape back armholes
Bind off 5 sts at beg of next 2 rows—56 (62, 68, 74) sts. Dec 1 st at each end of next row—54 (60, 66, 72) sts. Work even until armhole measures 3½ (4, 4½, 5)", end on wrong side ready for a k row.

Shape back shoulders
Bind off 7 (8, 9, 10) sts at beg of next 4 rows—26 (28, 30, 32) sts. ᶜl rem sts to holder for back of neck.

The front

Work in the same manner as the back until armhole measures ¼" deep, cut MC. Join CC and work even for 16 (18, 22, 24) rows, cut CC. Join MC and work even until armhole measures 2¾ (3, 3½, 3¾)", end on wrong side, ready for a k row.

Shape front neck
Divide work: K 14 (16, 18, 20), bind off next 26 (28, 30, 32) sts for center front neck edge, k rem sts—14 (16, 18, 20) sts each side.
Next row: P 14 (16, 18, 20), drop yarn, join another ball of MC and p rem 14 (16, 18, 20) sts.

Work even across both groups of sts each row until front armhole measures same as back, end on wrong side, ready for a k row.

Shape front shoulders
Working across both groups of sts each row, bind off 7 (8, 9, 10) sts at beg of next 4 rows. Fasten.

The sleeve

Instructions are given for both a puffed sleeve cap (girl's sweater) and a plain set-in sleeve cap (boy's or girl's sweater).

With smaller size needles and MC, cast on 45 (47, 50, 52) sts. Work in k 1, p 1 ribbing for 1", inc 12 sts evenly spaced across last rib row—57 (59, 62, 64) sts. Work even until sleeve measures 2 (2¼, 2½, 2¾)" from beg, end on wrong side ready for a k row.

Puffed sleeve cap only
Bind off 5 sts at beg of next 2 rows—47 (49, 52, 54) sts. Dec 1 st each end of next row—45 (47, 50, 52) sts. Work even until cap measures 2 (2½, 3, 3½)".
Dec row: K 2 tog, k 1, k 2 tog, k to last 5 sts, end k 2 tog, k 1, k 2 tog—2 sts taken off each end.
Next row: P across. Rep these 2 rows 7 times more—13 (15, 18, 20) sts.
Last row: K 2 tog across and bind off at the same time. Fasten.

Plain set-in sleeve cap only
Bind off 5 sts at beg of next 2 rows—47 (49, 52, 54) sts.
Single decrease row: K 1, SKP, k to last 3 sts, end k 2 tog, k 1—1 st taken off each end.
Next row: P across.
Rep these 2 rows 2 (2, 5, 8) times more—41 (43, 40, 36) sts.
Double decrease row: K 1, sl 2, k 1, pass both sl sts over, k to last 4 sts, end k 3 tog, k 1—2 sts taken off each end.
Next row: P across.
Rep these 2 rows 7 (7, 6, 5) times more—9 (11, 12, 12) sts. Bind off rem sts, fasten.

Cross stitch

Embroidering the horses

Following (HS) embroidery chart, with tapestry needle and six strands of embroidery floss, work the (HS) design in cross stitch. Each "X" of the cross stitch covers one "V" of the knitted fabric. Keep embroidery tension fairly slack to avoid bunching the fabric.

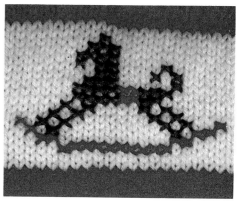

This close-up reveals that a properly executed cross stitch on the right side of the fabric shows up as a lone vertical on the wrong side. If you catch the loose ends of your working strand under a few embroidered stitches as you go, you will save having to weave them in later.

Close-up of the rocking horse panel. The white background is a knitted-in stockinette stitch stripe on the sweater front. Embroider the horses on before sewing the garment together, using six strands of shiny cotton embroidery floss and the cross stitch.

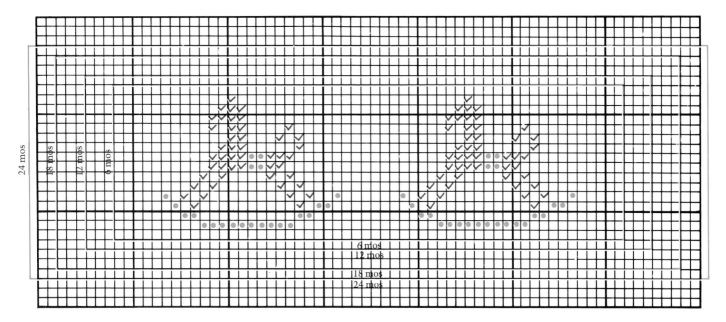

Each square of the graph represents a knitted stitch. Work cross stitch in horizontal rows, left to right or right to left. Each "X" of the cross stitch covers a "V" of the knitted fabric. All sizes have 2 embroidered rocking horses, 5 sts apart. The number of rows above and below, and stitches to the left and right of the design, increases from size to size. Note that for all sizes there is one stitch more to the right of the design than to the left. Count carefully in order to place the design correctly.

Finishing the garment

With tapestry needle and yarn, sew side, shoulder, and sleeve seams. Set in sleeves, gathering fullness of puffed sleeve cap at shoulder, or easing in fullness of plain set-in cap.

Back and side neck edging: With right side of work facing, MC, and smaller size needles, pick up 15 (16, 17, 18) sts along right front neck edge, k the 26 (28, 30, 32) sts of back neck edge from holder, pick up 15 (16, 17, 18) sts along left front neck edge—56 (60, 64, 68) sts. Working in k 1, p 1 ribbing, k tog the first and last 2 sts of every other row twice—52 (56, 60, 64) sts. Bind off loosely in ribbing.

Front neck edging: With right side of work facing, MC, and smaller size needles, pick up 1 st in each of 26 (28, 30, 32) bound-off sts of front neck edge. Working in k 1, p 1 ribbing, k tog the first and last 2 sts of every other row twice—22 (24, 26, 28) sts. Bind off in ribbing at even tension. Sew neck edging seams.

Make the edging conform to the square peasant's neck of the sweater by decreasing at the front corners to miter them.

Flowered Knit Dress

Our infant's dress is made of worsted-weight yarn so it knits up quickly. It is a happy combination of practicality and charm. The easy shape and generous skirt will fit babies of different weights. Also, when littlest girls are propped in a sitting position to receive visitors, the skirt conceals the slumpy-dumpy posture that even the prettiest babies just can't help. The dainty details make the difference: puffed sleeves, decorative horizontal bands of seed stitch and contrasting-color flowers, plus the smocked effect created by a ribbed band above the skirt. A button closure extends partway down the back.

From the hem to the armhole, the dress is worked on circular needles. If you're apprehensive about working in the round, this very, very small and pretty project is a good way to learn the advantages of circular knitting. For example: circular knitting is seamless, the right side of the work always faces you, and there is a minimum of purl stitches.

This pattern can also be used to make a knitted skirt by binding off after completing the ribbed band, folding the ribbing to the wrong side, stitching the ribbing down, and inserting ¼" elastic.

Flowered dress instructions are given for newborn-6 months size. Changes for 6 months-12 months size are in parentheses. The finished chest measurements are 21 (23)".

Shop for these items

Worsted weight yarn to knit the indicated gauge, in 4 colors (we used pink for MC, green and yellow for   , white for background); 3½ oz (100 gr) MC and ½ oz (14 gr) of each CC .

Circ knitting needles, one 29" size 5 and one 24" size 3 (or one 29" in the size that gives you the correct gauge, and one 24" two sizes smaller).

Crochet hook size E or F.
4 st holders.
A tapestry needle.
4¼" buttons.

Correct gauge is important

Working in St st: 5 sts = 1", 7 rows = 1". To ensure the correct finished measurements, take time to check gauge by making a sample swatch: With the larger size needle, cast on 20 sts. Work for 28 rows in St st. Lay swatch flat and measure it—without bunching or stretching, swatch should be 4" square. If swatch is too small, try again with larger needles; if it is too large, try smaller needles.

Body of dress

Skirt

Beg at lower edge, with larger needle loosely cast on 156 (164) sts. Place marker for beg of rnds and join, being careful not to twist sts. Work 4 rnds seed st, 6 rnds St st, 2 rnds seed st, 2 rnds St st. Cut MC.

✿ Panel for skirt

Note: Stranding is the technique of working with more than one color across a row, as in the ✿ panel of our knitted dress. Carry yarns at even tension across the wrong side of work, overlapping them by bringing the strand of color in current use under or over the strand of color previously used. The photo detail of the wrong side of ✿ panel shows the yarns overlapped every 3rd or 4th st.

✿ Bed: Join green and work 2 rnds in St st, dec 4 sts evenly spaced on the first rnd—152 (160) sts.

✿ Stems: Join white, k 3 white, * k 1 tbl green, k 7 white, rep from * 17 (18) times more, end k 1 tbl green, k 4 white. Rep this row once more.

✿ Leaves: K 1 white, * insert crochet hk under horizontal strand to the right of nearest green (stem) st of previous row,

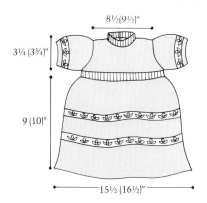

yo with green, draw green lp through to front of work and transfer to right needle, k 2 white, k 1 tbl green, k 2 white, insert crochet hk under horizontal strand to the left of last green (stem) st, yo with green, draw green lp through to front of work and transfer to right needle, k 3 white, rep from * around, end last rep with k 2 white. Cut green—190 (200) sts.

Next rnd: With white, * k tog first white and first green st, k 2 white sts, k tbl 1 green st, k 2 white sts, k tbl tog next green and next white st, k 1 white st, rep from * around—152 (160) sts.

✿ Tops: K 3 white, join yellow, * yellow bobble in next st as foll: (k in the front and the back of st) twice, pass the first,

2nd, and 3rd sts over the 4th st and off right needle, k 7 white, rep from * around, end last rep with k 4. Cut yellow.

Last rnd: With white, k around. This completes ✿ panel. Cut white.

Join MC. Work 2 rnds St st, 2 rnds seed st, 7 rnds St st, 2 rnds seed st, 2 rnds St st, cut MC. Rep ✿ Panel for skirt once. Join MC, work 2 rnds St st, 2 rnds seed st, then work even in St st until work measures 9 (10)" from beg or desired length to underarm, less 1 (1¼)".

Dec Rnd: * K 1, k 2 tog, rep from * around, end k 2 (1)—102 (107) sts.

Ribbing: Change to smaller needle. Work k 1, p 1 ribbing for 1 (1¼)", dec (inc) 2 (3) sts evenly spaced across last rib row—100 (110) sts. Change to larger needle and k 1 rnd.

Divide work for backs and front: Turn work and p 21 (23) sts (right back), place the 21 (23) sts for right back on st holder, bind off next 8 (8) sts (right armhole), p next 41 (47) sts (front), place the 42 (48) sts for front on a 2nd st holder, bind off next 8 (8) sts (left armhole), p next 20 (22) sts (left back)—there are 21 (23) sts rem on needle for left back.

This is the right side of the ✿ panel. The stem stitches are raised by twisting them (knitting through the back loop of the stitch). Each leaf is formed by drawing a loop of green yarn through and across the fabric. The raised, rounded flower tops are bobbles knitted with yellow yarn into the top stem stitch.

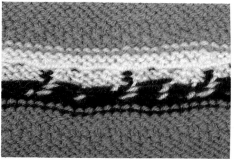

This is the wrong side of the ✿ panel. The strands of yarn are carried across the back of the work at even tension to prevent puckering. The yarns are overlapped every third or fourth stitch to keep the fabric flat and neat.

This is the panel in progress. Each leaf is formed by drawing a loop of green yarn through the fabric from close to the stem stitches diagonally up and across several rows with a crochet hook. The loop is then transferred to the right knitting needle. Note that the right leaf emerges from a point one row lower than the left leaf.

Backs

Shape left back armhole: Working only on the 21 (23) sts of left back, dec 1 st at armhole edge every other row 4 times—17 (19) sts. Work even until armhole measures 3¼ (3¾)", ending at armhole edge.

Shape the left back shoulder: Bind off 5 (6) sts at beg of next row, work 1 row even—12 (13) sts. Rep these 2 rows once—7 (7) sts. Place rem 7 sts on st holder for left back neck.

Shape the right back armhole and shoulder: Sl 21 (23) sts of right back from st holder to needle. Join MC and follow instructions for left back armhole and shoulder. Place rem 7 sts on st holder for right back neck.

Front

Shape front armholes: Sl the 42 (48) sts for front from st holder to needle, join MC. Dec 1 st each end every other row 4 times—34 (40) sts. Work even until armhole measures 2¼ (2¾)", ending at right armhole ready for a p row.

Shape the front neck: P across first 14 (16) sts of next row, place next 6 (8) sts on st holder for center front neck, join another ball of MC and P rem 14 (16) sts. Work across both sides of neck for each foll row. K across first 14 (16) sts of next row (left side of neck), drop yarn, pick up second strand, bind off first 2 sts of right side of neck, k rem sts—12 (14) sts on left side of neck. P across left side of neck, drop yarn, pick up second strand, bind off first 2 sts of right side of neck, p rem sts—12 (14) sts on each side of neck. Dec 1 st at each neck edge every other row twice—10 (12) sts on each side of neck. Work even until front armhole measures same as back.

Shape the front shoulders: Bind off 5 (6) sts at beg of next 4 rows, fasten.

The sleeve

With smaller size needles and MC, cast on 26 (30) sts. Work 4 rows seed st. K all sts of next row, inc 12 sts evenly spaced across—38 (42) sts. Change to larger needles. P 1 row. Cut MC.

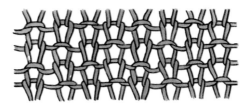

Seed stitch

♣ Panel for sleeve

♣ Bed: Join green and k 1 row, inc 6 (8) sts evenly spaced across—44 (50) sts. P 1 row.

♣ Stems: Join white, k 6 (9) white, * k 1 tbl green, k 7 white, rep from * 4 times more, end last rep k 5 (8) white.
Next row: P 5 (8) white, * p 1 tbl green, p 7 white, rep from * 4 times more, end last rep p 6 (9) white.
♣ Leaves: K 4 (7) white, * insert crochet hk under horizontal strand to the right of nearest green (stem) st of previous row, yo with green, draw green lp through to front of work and transfer to right needle, k 2 white, k 1 tbl green, k 2 white, insert crochet hk under horizontal strand to the left of last green (stem) st, yo with green, draw green lp through to front of work and transfer to right needle, rep from * across, end last rep k 3 (6) white. Cut green—54 (60) sts.
Next row: With white, * p 2 (5), p tog next white and first green st, p 2 white sts, p tbl 1 green st, p 2 white sts, p tog next green and next white st, p 1 white st, rep from * across, end last rep p 3 (6) white—44 (50) sts.
♣ Tops: K 6 (9) white, join yellow, * yellow bobble in next st, k 7 white, rep from * across, end last rep k 5 (8) white. Cut yellow.
Last row: P across in white. Cut white. This completes ♣ panel.

Join MC, work 2 rows St st, 2 rows seed st, then work even in St st until sleeve measures 3" from beg or desired length to underarm.

Shape the sleeve cap

Bind off 4 sts at beg of next 2 rows—36 (42) sts. Dec 1 st each end every other row 4 (6) times—28 (30) sts. K 2 tog across next row and bind off at the same time.

Finishing the garment

With tapestry needle and MC, sew shoulder and sleeve seams. Set in sleeves, easing in fullness at cap.

Neck border: With right side facing, smaller size needles, and MC, pick up about 66 (70) sts around neck edge, including sts on holders. Work k 1, p 1 ribbing for 4 rows. Bind off loosely in ribbing.

Button border: With right side of work facing, crochet hk, and MC, work 1 row of evenly spaced sc along left edge of back opening, ch 1, turn. Sl st in each sc across, fasten.

Buttonloop border: Sl st along right edge of back opening, making 4 evenly spaced buttonloops as foll: (ch 5, sl st in st at base of ch 5) for each lp. Sew on buttons opposite buttonloops.

This is the back opening and neck edge of the completed dress. Note that the buttonloops extend from the edge of the opening. This causes the edges of the opening to butt rather than overlap when the dress is fastened.

5.

*Heirloom Gifts
and Toys*

Three Cross-Stitch Designs

Pig
Duck
Name Hanging

Instructions for three small cross-stitch embroidery designs follow. Two of them, the pig and duck, were worked on aida cloth and framed as pictures. The third is a design made around a child's name, worked on linen and finished as a little hanging for the carriage, crib, or nursery door.

A well-scrubbed, prize pink pig poses with feet firmly planted, with majestic corpulence. His ears are pricked up in alert intelligence as if his attention has just been drawn to a delicacy just beyond the picture plane. Around his neck is an appetizing garland of shiny apples, as round and cheerful as he.

The duck family is embroidered in the bright colors that children respond to. Mama duck is teaching her two little ones to get around in the water. As she instructs the duckling at her side, the other one leaps through the air in a daring dive that makes the cattails vibrate.

We photographed the name hanging together with the quilted bunting and carriage blanket. If you turn to that picture, you will see it as a sort of license plate on the front of a beautiful antique wicker carriage. Two branches, embroidered in magenta and blue-green, form the borders of the design. The child's name is embroidered in the center, in yellow capital letters. The hanging is edged with cotton cord piping and backed with felt.

PIG AND DUCK

One finished picture measures 7½ x 10" in the frame. Fabric measurements include 3" allowance all around for fraying and framing. Each design is embroidered entirely in cross stitch.

Shop for these items

Aida cloth or other even weave or even weave-squared fabric that will give you 7 stitches per inch, 1 piece 14 x 16" for each design.

Six-strand embroidery floss.

For pig, 1 skein each medium green, dark green, very dark green, light pink, medium pink, dark pink, very dark pink, yellow, black, white, and gray.

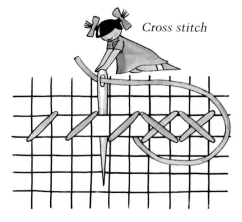
Cross stitch

For duck, 1 skein each medium green, dark green, medium pink, light blue, medium dark blue, yellow, sienna, black, white, and gray.

Embroidery needle.

Embroidering the design

Work with 2 strands of embroidery floss. Mark center of fabric. Find the center of the chart. Following the chart, begin work from the center and embroider back and forth across each color area. All bottom stitches should slant in one direction. All top stitches should slant the opposite way. When you have completed one half of the embroidery, turn your work and the chart around and finish the picture in the opposite direction. As you work, catch the loose ends under the embroidered stitches on the wrong side, and you will save having to weave them in later. The finished picture can be framed, or made into a pillow or small hanging.

NAME HANGING

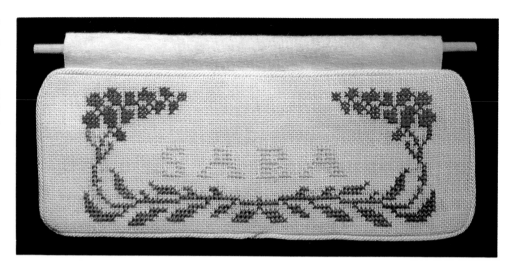

The finished name hanging measures about 10½ x 3¾". Fabric measurements include a 1½" seam allowance. The design is embroidered in cross stitch.

Shop for these items

Even weave linen or other fabric about 18 threads per inch, 1 piece 13½ x 6¾", white or desired color.
Felt for backing, 1 piece 13½ x 8", white or desired color.
Pre-made cotton cord piping, 30", white or desired color.
Six-strand embroidery floss, 1 skein each blue-green, magenta, and yellow, or desired colors.
Cotton sewing thread to match fabric.
Graph paper.

Embroidering the border

Use 4 strands of embroidery floss throughout. Mark center of fabric. Following the chart, work the border design as shown, beginning at midpoint of lower edge. The embroidery should extend to 1¾" from the raw edges. Turn work around, return to starting point on chart and fabric, and repeat the design in the opposite direction.

Embroidering the name

Refer to the small charted alphabet in chapter VI. Sketch out on graph paper the child's name so that it will fit onto the central space of fabric within the embroidered border. Each square of the graph represents a cross-stitch space. Each embroidered cross stitch covers 2 x 2 threads of fabric. Count the number of threads your design will cover horizontally and vertically, and draw placement lines on the fabric with a soft pencil. Embroider.

Blue-green ❏❏❏   Magenta ◎◎◎

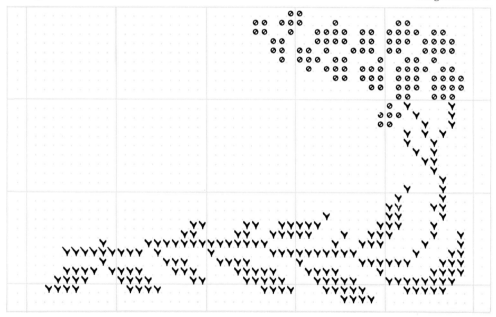

Assembling the hanging

Position the piping around the edges of the right side of the embroidered fabric, slightly rounding the corners of the square. Piped edge should be facing in, and piping seamline should lie on the fabric seam allowance line. Machine-baste ¼" above seamline.

Lay the backing felt over the piping and fabric, matching lower and side edges, right sides together. Stitch around 3 sides, leaving top open. Clip corners and trim seam allowance to ½". Extend the felt out from the top edge, and make 2 vertical cuts from felt edge to piping to narrow the flap about ¾" on either side. Fold the flap over towards the back and tuck the end inside. Trim and tuck inside excess felt on either side of flap. Topstitch all around hanging between piping and linen.

Victorian Squeeze Ball

We knew toys aren't supposed to be practical, but the antique Victorian Squeeze Ball (it's too large to be called a clutch ball) can double as a pillow for those brief periods of enervation in the day of an otherwise tireless infant. Its Victorian lineage is revealed by the fancy-stitched seams and pentagonal patchwork. By scaling the pentagons up or down, you could make a bigger or smaller ball.

Completed toy measures about 18″ around.

Shop for these items

Fabric scraps in various colors.
Embroidery floss in various colors.
Sewing thread.
Embroidery and sewing needles.
Polyester fiberfill.
Tracing or tissue paper.
Dressmaker's carbon paper.

Making the pentagons

Trace the pentagon from these pages (includes ¼″ seam allowance) and transfer it 12 times to fabric scraps; cut out. Press edges of each pentagon under ¼″ and baste.

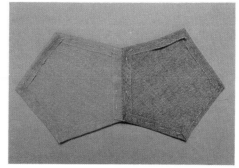

Wrong side view of two joined pentagons. The edges of each piece are turned under ¼″, pressed, and basted. The folded edges are joined from the right side with tiny, invisible slip-stitches. This method is used to piece together the fabric of all three squeeze toys.

Joining and embroidering

With right sides up, slip-stitch the pentagons together in 2 groups of six. Surround one pentagon with five; sew one edge of each of the five to each edge of the center shape. Sew the edges of the five together to form 2 hemispheres of fabric. Using three strands of floss, decorate the seams of each hemisphere with various embroidery stitches. Slip-stitch the two hemispheres together, embroidering along the new seams as you go. When the joinings are nearly finished, stuff ball. Slip-stitch closed and embroider over the last seams. Remove basting threads.

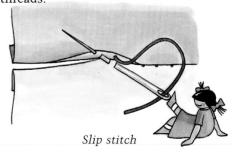

Slip stitch

Have-a-Heart

What is parenthood, or aunthood, or unclehood, siblinghood, friendhood, etc; but the giving of one's heart, trustingly, again and again. To symbolize this never depleted resource, we invite you to make a soft patchwork heart. Its securely joined fragments of fabric represent the adult's heart, which has been broken time and time again through life, but always emerged the stronger for it. We call it the Have-a-Heart. It will bounce back from every squeeze!

F inished heart measures about 5¾" across at widest point.

Shop for these items
Fabric scraps in various colors.
Sewing thread.
Polyester fiberfill.
Tracing or tissue paper.
Dressmaker's carbon paper.

Cutting and joining
Trace separately each triangular fragment and its number within the heart from the pattern diagram, adding ¼" seam allowance around each shape. Trace the outermost outline of the heart (includes seam allowance). Transfer all shapes and number to fabric; cut out.

Press edges of small shapes under ¼", excepting edges that will form the outer edge of the heart when pieces are joined. Stitch down with small running stitches. Referring to the pattern diagram, slip-stitch the sections together, right sides up, to form the heart shape.

Place the two hearts with right sides together; sew seam ¼" from edge. leaving an opening for turning and stuffing. Turn right side out and stuff. Stitch opening closed.

The triangular fragments of the heart front are slip-stitched in the same manner as the pentagons of the Victorian Squeeze Ball. Instead of holding the edges under with basting sitches that are later removed, we used small, even running stitches that become part of the design.

Soft Little Bear

Practice the old-fashioned, intricate hand-basting and slip-stitching that still produce the best, most perfectly joined quilts, by making this tiny toy bear. One side is patchwork, and the other side is cut from a single piece of fabric. If you're an experienced quilter, you won't need to follow our pattern to piece your fabric together. If you're unenthusiastic about patchwork, cut both sides from solid fabric. Embroidered running stitches set off the ears and arms and make them more bendable. You might want to embroider the features as well.

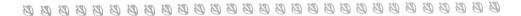

Soft bear measures about 7¼" high when finished.

Shop for these items
Fabric scraps in various colors.
Embroidery floss in various colors.
Sewing thread.
Embroidery and sewing needles.
Polyester fiberfill.
Tracing or tissue paper.
Dressmaker's carbon paper.

Cutting and joining
Trace separately each triangular fragment and its number within the bear outline from the pattern diagram, adding ¼" seam allowance all around each shape. Trace the outermost outline of the bear (includes seam allowance). Transfer all shapes and numbers to fabric; cut out.

Press edges of small shapes under ¼", excepting edges that will form the outer edge of the bear when pieces are joined; baste. Referring to the pattern diagram, slip-stitch the sections together, right sides up, to form the front of the bear.

Place the two halves of the bear with right sides together; sew seam ¼" from edge, leaving an opening for turning and stuffing. Turn right side out and stuff. Stitch opening closed.

Using 2 strands of embroidery floss, work lines of tight running stitches as indicated on pattern diagram to define arms and ears. Tie a ribbon bow around neck.

The triangular fragments of the bear front are basted and slip-stitched in the same manner as the pentagons of the Victorian Squeeze Ball. After the bear is sewn and stuffed, the ears and arms are set off with lines of running stitches, using 2 strands of embroidery floss.

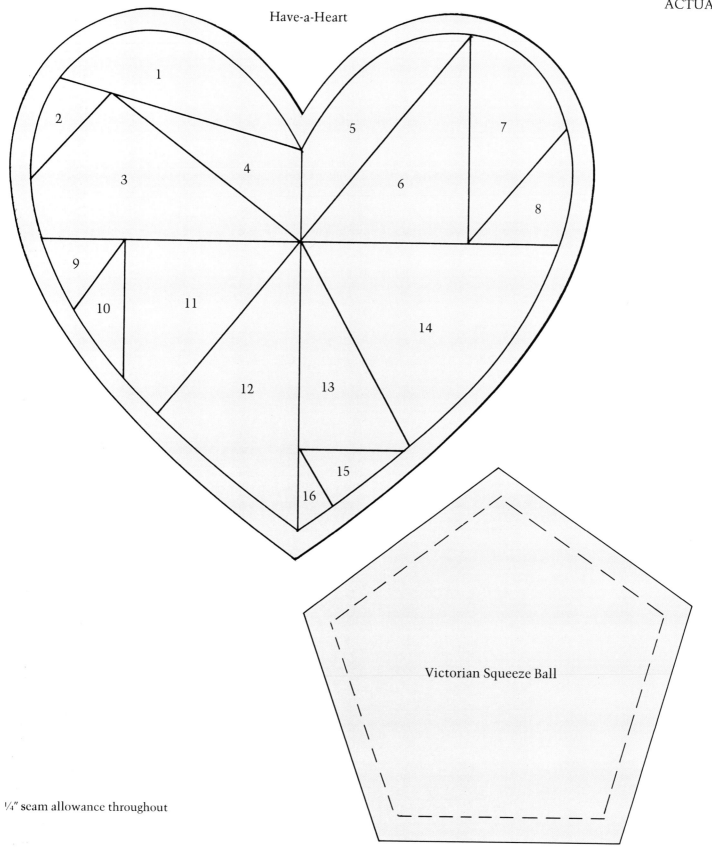

Have-a-Heart

Victorian Squeeze Ball

¼″ seam allowance throughout

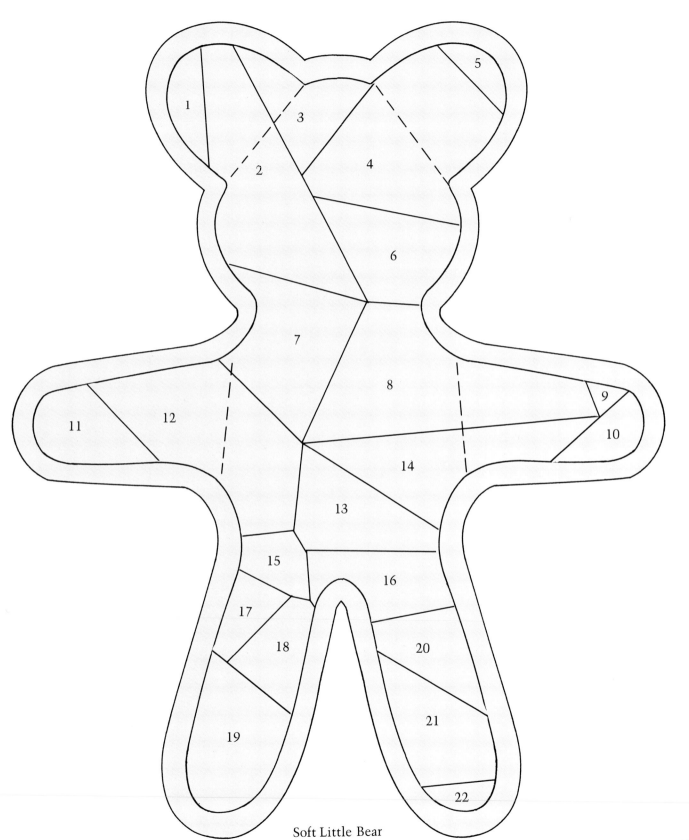

Soft Little Bear

Topsy-turvy Doll

There are journeys that only the imagination can take. The moon isn't made of green cheese. Real grass isn't pink. Animals don't talk, and real people don't have a head at either end. All the more reason, say we, that in our creative fantasies and endeavors we should re-tint the foliage, put words in animal's mouths, give dolls as many heads as necessary, and imagine heavenly bodies to consist of whatever edible or non-edible porous substance we prefer.

The topsy-turvy doll is designed to live in a child's topsy-turvy world, where the iron-clad rules of science and nature have not yet established complete control; where adults are forever doing unexplainable things and only the behavior of imaginary playmates makes sense. A flip of the doll, and one friend disappears beneath the skirt. A new friend, temporarily forgotten, different in looks and personality, appears—the way a new, unsuspected world materializes when one opens a book or enters one's dreams.

This black-white doll design is patterned after an American colonial antique. It is made entirely of fabric and yarn, and is stuffed with fiberfill. You might have enough scraps in your sewing basket to make the entire project. The clothing and hair are securely sewn on and the facial features are embroidered. Only the aprons are removable. The black doll's blouse has cuffs and a high neckband; her apron has a neckstrap. The pink doll has a lace collar.

If you are a quilter, you might want to piece together the fabric for one or both doll's dresses. If you like to embroider, decorate the aprons with fancy stitches. If you construct this doll with durability in mind, and repair it carefully when necessary, it ought to withstand the most emphatically loving treatment.

From head to head, the finished doll measures about 9". The seam allowances are ¼". The faces are embroidered with running stitch, satin stitch, stem stitch, straight stitch, and French knots.

Shop for these items

Fabric remnants
For doll bodies, 1 20 x 6" or 10 x 12" piece each light pink and black or dark brown.
For doll dresses, 1 10 x 36" piece for each dress (we used a blue floral print for the pink doll's dress and solid red for the black doll's dress).
For aprons, 1 10 x 16" piece for both (we used white).
Lace, 1" wide strip, 6" long.
White felt, small scrap.
Sewing thread to match fabrics.
Six-strand embroidery floss, 1 skein each red, brown, pale blue, black.
Yarn scraps for hair (we used 2-ply acrylic), gold and black or desired colors.
1 embroidery needle.
Dressmaker's carbon paper.
Tissue or tracing paper (to make pattern).
Polyester fiberfill.

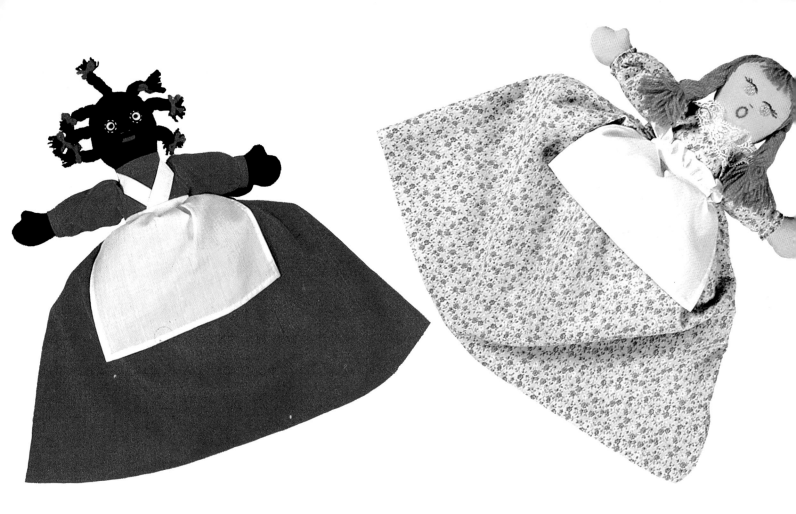

Cutting and marking the fabric

Enlarge and trace pattern pieces onto tissue paper. Transfer all markings. Cut out paper pattern. Pin body and arm pieces to fabric. Transfer all markings and cut out 2 upper bodies and 4 arms in each color. For dresses, cut 2 pieces 10 x 28" of each fabric for skirts, 2 pieces 3 x 5" of each fabric for sleeves, and 2 bodices (according to pattern piece) of each fabric, transferring all markings. For aprons, cut 2 pieces 5 x 7", 2 strips 1 x 16", and one strip 1½ x 9".

Topsy-turvy body

Sew each pink body to a black body along the lower edge. Place the 2 body sections right sides together, matching colors. Sew seam, leaving an opening for turning and stuffing. Turn right side out and stuff. Place right sides together of each pair of pink and black arm pieces. Sew seam, leaving upper arm end open. Turn

right side out and stuff. Gather fabric and stitch to close upper arm ends. Refer to pattern markings and sew arms to torso.

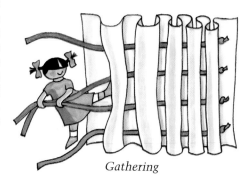

Gathering

Topsy-turvy faces

All embroidery is done with three strands of embroidery floss. With a soft pencil or piece of chalk, sketch in the placement of the facial features, following the diagram. To make the pink doll face, outline the eyelids with brown

stem stitch and make eyelashes with straight stitches at each outer end. Embroider each eye with a closely worked pale blue spiral of stem stitch beginning at the center. The mouth is a red oval of stem stitch and the nose is a single straight stitch of the same red.

To make the black doll face, cut 2 small circles of white felt and anchor them to the head with black French knots. Outline the eyes in a running stitch of white sewing thread. The mouth is a horizontal bar of red satin stitches. Two small vertical stitches in the center hold down the satin stitches and divide them into upper and lower lips. The nose is made with 2 straight stitches of red.

Topsy-turvy hairdos

For the pink doll head, cut about 100 strands 10" long of the gold yarn. Center the strands of hair and lay them across

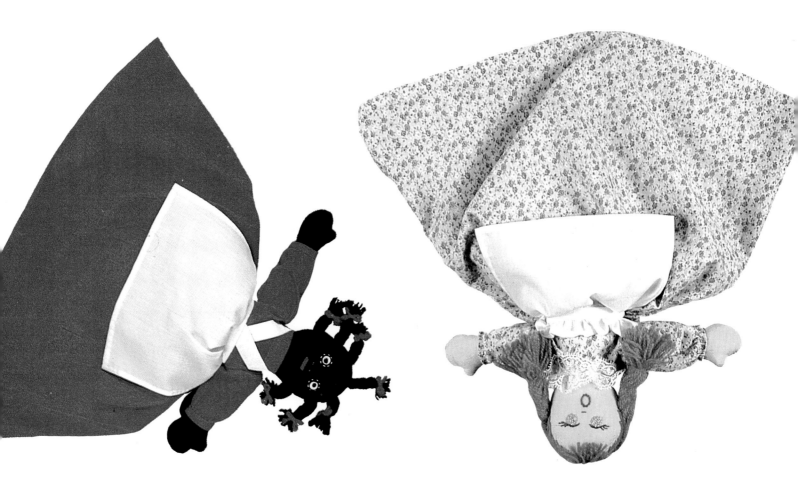

the head one at a time, starting at top seam line and working down back of head. Using an embroidery needle threaded with one strand of the same yarn, backstitch the hair down as you go, in a line down the center back of the head ending about ³⁄₈" from nape of neck. Make into 2 braids. Cut about 12 strands 2" long, double them over, and tack them down to the center top of head, extending them from the hairline over the forehead to form bangs.

For the black doll head, cut 56 strands 10" long (8 strands for each braid). Thread 8 strands through a needle with a large eye and a sharp point. Beginning at about the level of the mouth insert needle into fabric of head near seam and bring it out again close to the same spot. Pull the yarn halfway through (16 strands now emerging from head). Make a braid about 1" long. Tie braid securely with red yarn

and trim the excess yarn. Repeat to make 7 braids all around the head seam. If you wish, add braids to back of head as well.

This is the back of the pink doll-head. One at a time, strands of 2-ply yarn are laid across the head from forehead to nape of neck, and sewn in with a backstitch using the same yarn. The bangs are shorter strands, doubled and also anchored on with backstitch.

SKIRT

1. Place the 2 10 x 28" skirt pieces of different fabrics with right sides together. Stitch along one long edge. Open out joined fabrics and press seam open. Fold over across the seam so that each fabric is folded onto itself with right sides facing. Sew the long edges together, leaving 3" open at either end. Turn right side out. You now have a long flat tube, half of one fabric and half of the other, and open at either end.

2. Run two gathering threads around each open end of the tube of fabric. Slip tube over doll. Bunch open ends of fabric together at waist, with raw edges extending in opposite directions towards doll heads. Pull gathers tight at waistline. Now the tube has shut up into a reversible gathered skirt. Sew gathered edges to doll body.

BLOUSE

1. Slit bodices up the center back and 1" across the neck as marked on pattern.

2. Run a gathering thread across one long edge of each sleeve, and gather to fit between bodice armhole markings. Sew in sleeves. Turn cuff edge under ¼" twice and hem. Sew side and sleeve seams.

3. Fold center back edges of blouses under ¼" and press. Put blouses on doll to match skirts. Slip-stitch center back seam.

4. Turn lower edge of bodice under and slip-stitch to skirt, concealing the gathering threads.

5. Run gathering threads around sleeve cuff edges, fasten sleeves to doll wrists. Slip-stitch sleeve to wrist fabric.

6. Stitch a piece of lace to the neck and dress fabric of the pink doll.

7. Cut a 1½ x 5½" strip of fabric to match the black doll's dress. Fold each long edge over scant ½" and press. Turn

ends under and press. Position around neck of black doll, overlapping raw edge of fabric. Slip-stitch to neck and dress fabric. Cut 2 1 x 3½" strips of same fabric. Fold and stitch around wrists over sleeve gathers in same manner.

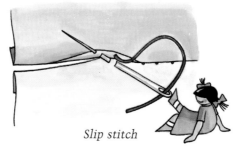

Slip stitch

APRONS

1. Fold 1½ x 9" strip of white fabric in same manner as neck and wrist bands. Place around black doll's neck and cross in front. Sew ends to bodice at waistline.

2. Turn 3 edges of a 7 x 5" apron bib piece under ¼" twice and hem, leaving one long edge unhemmed. Run a gathering thread along the unhemmed edge. Gather to 3¼" width.

3. Turn ends of one 1 x 16" strip under and fold like the other long strips. Position apron in center of strip, enclosing the raw gathered edge in the fold. Stitch from one end of the strip to the other. Tie apron on black doll.

A high neckband on the dress and a neck-strap on the apron of the black doll differentiate the two doll outfits. They are made by folding narrow strips of matching fabric in thirds, to conceal the raw edges.

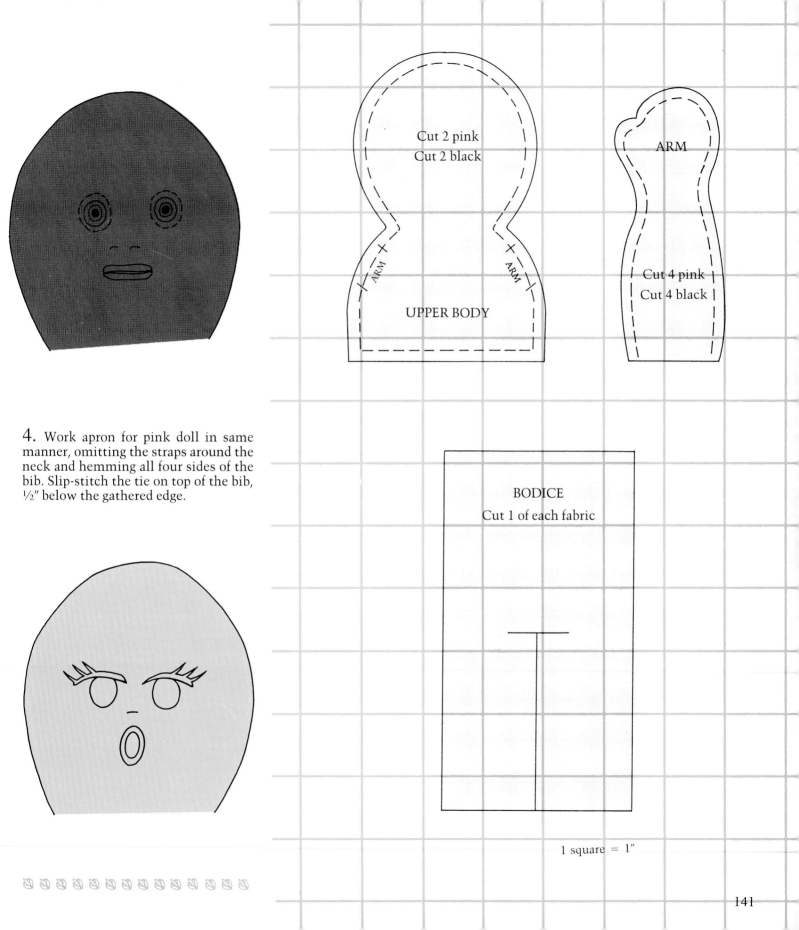

Cut 2 pink
Cut 2 black

ARM

ARM

ARM

UPPER BODY

Cut 4 pink
Cut 4 black

BODICE
Cut 1 of each fabric

1 square = 1"

4. Work apron for pink doll in same manner, omitting the straps around the neck and hemming all four sides of the bib. Slip-stitch the tie on top of the bib, ½" below the gathered edge.

6.

Appendix

Needlework Techniques, Terms and Helpful Information

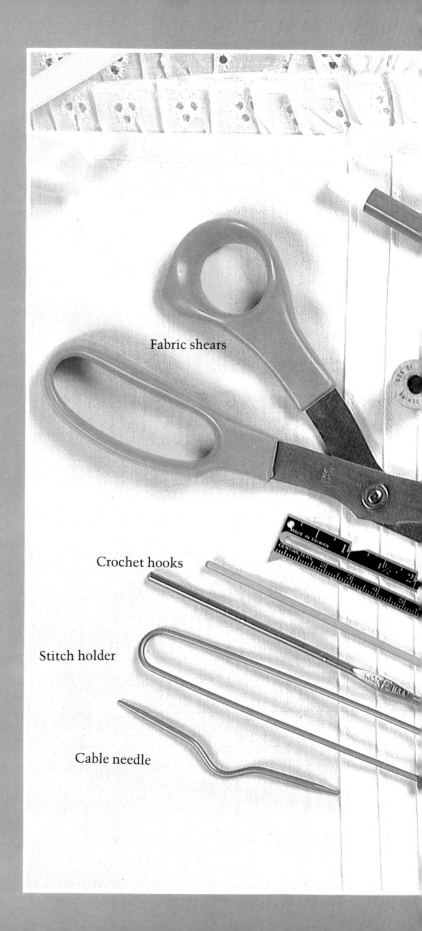

Fabric shears

Crochet hooks

Stitch holder

Cable needle

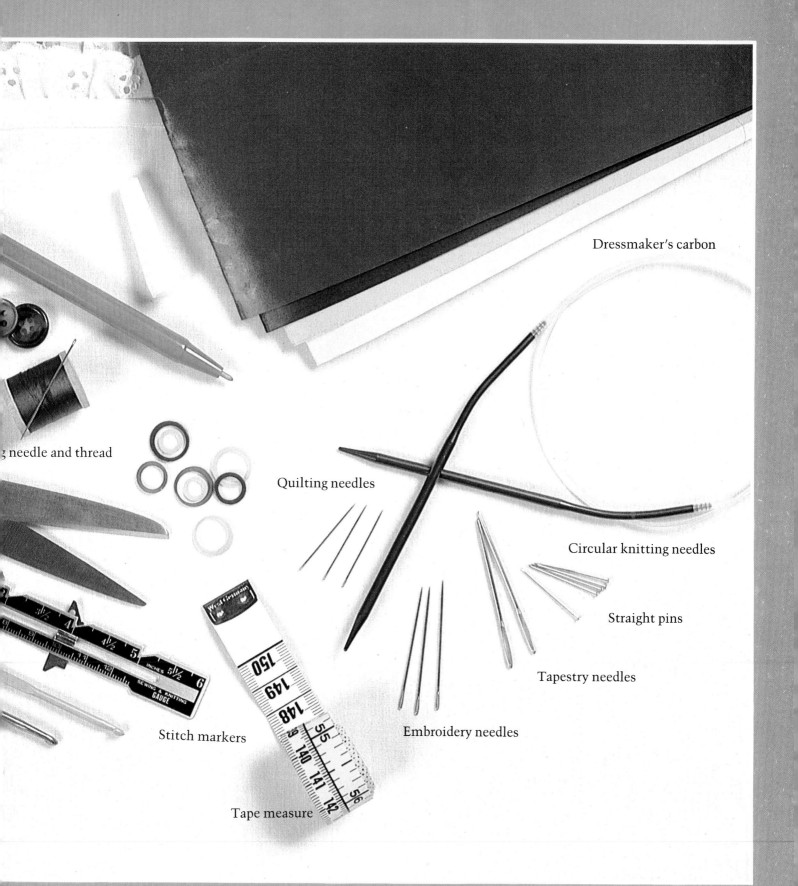

Dressmaker's carbon

needle and thread

Quilting needles

Circular knitting needles

Straight pins

Tapestry needles

Stitch markers

Embroidery needles

Tape measure

Marking and Gathering

Marking and Gathering Fabric for Smocking

1. Mark the wrong side of the fabric with rows of dots from an iron-on dot transfer. Thread your needle with button or carpet thread. Make rows of even running stitches, using the dots as your guide. Knot one end of the thread and leave the other end free.

2. Hold the gathering threads and bunch up the fabric into folds. Fasten the free ends of thread to hold the folds in place.

Marking the Center of Fabric for Embroidery

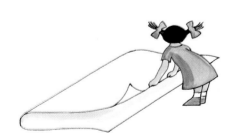  

1. Fold fabric in half and crease along the fold.

2. Fold in half again and crease.

3. Open fabric and mark it on the right side where the creases intersect.

Embroidery

Four-sided Stitch

1. Bring the needle up through the fabric at one corner of the square. Make a straight stitch along one side of the square, and bring the needle up at the corner diagonally opposite.

2. Make a second straight stitch to meet the first stitch in an "L" and again bring the needle up at the corner diagonally opposite.

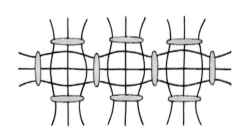

3. Make a third straight stitch to meet the first stitch in a "U" and again bring the needle up at the corner diagonally opposite.

4. The last stitch of previous square is the first stitch of the next square. Pull each stitch firmly.

5. Finished four-sided stitches.

Cross Stitch

Cross stitch is always worked on an even weave fabric. Unless otherwise indicated, it should be embroidered over 2 X 2 threads. Establish the first half of each "X" across your row, working from left to right. Insert the needle vertically. Come back across the row and embroider the top half of the X. All bottom stitches should lie at one angle, all top stitches at the opposite angle.

Blanket Stitch

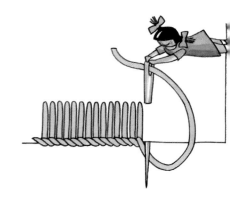

Satin Stitch

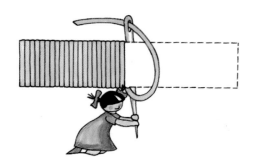

Insert the needle at a slight angle to make vertical stitches that wrap around the threads of fabric. This stitch is used both for surface embroidery and pulled-thread work.

Lazy Daisy Stitch

French Knot

1. Bring the needle up through the fabric to start the stitch. Wind the thread tautly once or twice around the needle.

2. Bring the needle down through the fabric next to where you come up to start the stitch. For a bolder effect double the thread.

Split Stitch

1. Make a stitch. Bring the needle up through the fabric, piercing the center of the stitch.

Start the stitch by bringing the needle up through the fabric close to the edge. Working from left to right, insert needle down through fabric at desired stitch length from the edge and pull needle out from edge, making a loop below the needle. Pull the loop taut with the emerging strand on top of it. Keep stitches at an even tension to lay flat along the fabric edge. This is also known as buttonhole stitch.

Back Stitch

Bring the needle up and insert it to the right a stitch length away. Bring needle out at the left a stitch length ahead. Keep stitches even. Back stitch is used in hand sewing, surface embroidery and in cross stitch embroidery to make outlines and contours. In cross stitch it is worked on an even weave fabric, usually over 2 threads at a time.

Stem Stitch

Bring the needle up through the fabric and insert it back down close to the same spot, making a loop. Pull loop to desired size and anchor it at the bottom with a small straight stitch. This can be worked as a single stitch or placed in groups.

Insert needle from right to left, bringing it out where the last stitch went in. Keep the thread below the needle.

2. Bring the needle down through the fabric, half a stitch length beyond the last pierced stitch. Split stitch looks like a delicate chain stitch and is good for outlining.

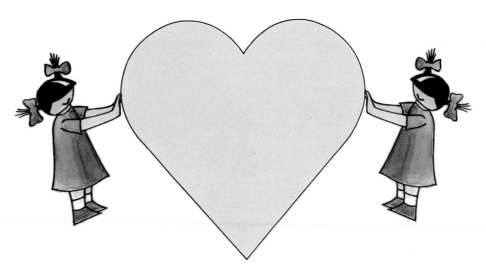

147

Sewing and Quilting

Knitting

Slip-stitch

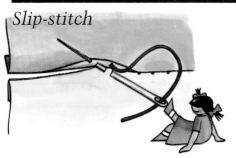

These are tiny stitches that alternate from one folded edge to another to make an invisible join. Use slip-stitch to piece fabric scraps together, or to close openings for turning and stuffing.

Quilting or Running Stitch

Weave the needle in and out of the fabric several times, and pull through, keeping the stitches small and even. This is used in quilting and hand sewing.

Yarn Over (yo)

Wrap yarn over the right hand needle without working into a stitch.

Knit (k)

With yarn in back of work, insert right needle behind left needle up through front of stitch, wrap yarn behind and under right needle and draw through stitch; slip stitch off left needle.

Purl (p)

With yarn in front of work, insert right needle in front of left needle down through front of stitch, wrap yarn over and behind right needle and draw through stitch; slip stitch off left needle.

Increase #1 (inc)

Knit into the front loop and into the back loop of the same stitch.

Increase #2 (inc)

Knit into the stitch of the row below the next stitch on the left needle.

Binding Off

Work 2 stitches,* lift the former stitch over the latter stitch and off the right needle, work the next stitch and repeat from* to end. Cut yarn and draw through the last remaining loop.

Decrease #1 (dec)

Knit 2 Together (K 2 tog)

This decrease slants to the right. Insert the right needle through 2 stitches at the same time and knit as if they were one stitch.

Decrease #2 (dec)

Slip-knit-pass (SKP)

This decrease slants to the left. Slip one stitch from the left to the right needle as if to knit, knit the next stitch, pass the slipped stitch over the knitted stitch and off the right needle.

Weaving Seams

Work back and forth from one edge to the other. Keeping in a straight line, bring the needle under 2 threads at a time. Seams should be elastic. Use a needle with a blunt point to avoid splitting the yarn.

Stockinette Stitch (St st)

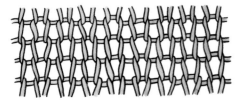

Knit side

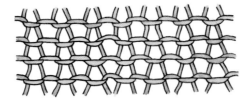

Purl side

Row 1: Knit. Row 2: Purl. Repeat these 2 rows. The knit side is smooth and looks like a series of connected V's. The purl side is pebbly and tends to curl under at the edges.

Seed Stitch

Picking up Stitches along Row Ends

Draw loops of yarn through stitches at row ends at regular intervals and place on needle.

Row 1: Knit 1, purl 1 across. Row 2: Knit the purl stitches and purl the knit stitches. Repeat row 2. Both sides of the fabric look the same.

1/1 Ribbing

Picking up Stitches along Bound-off or Cast-on Edges

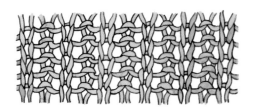

Draw loops of yarn through stitches near edge, skipping spaces between stitches, and place on needle.

Row 1: Knit 1, purl 1 across. Row 2: Knit the knit stitches and purl the purl stitches. Repeat row 2. Both sides of the fabric look the same.

Crocheting

Chain Stitch (ch)

Make a slip knot and place on hook.
*Yarn over hook and draw through loop, repeat from *.

Single Crochet (sc)

1. Insert hook into stitch, yarn over hook and draw through stitch. There are 2 loops on the hook.

2. Yarn over hook and draw through both loops on hook. There is one loop left

Half double crochet (hdc)

1. Yarn over hook, insert hook through stitch, yarn over hook and draw through stitch. You will have 3 loops on the hook.

2. Yarn over hook and draw through all 3 loops. You will have one loop left on the hook.

Double Crochet (dc)

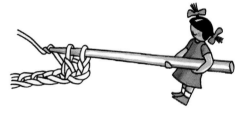

1. Yarn over hook, insert hook through stitch, yarn over hook and draw through stitch. You will have 3 loops on the hook.

2. Yarn over hook and draw through 2 loops. You will have 2 loops on the hook.

3. Yarn over hook and draw through the remaining 2 loops. You will have one loop left on the hook.

Knitting and Crochet Abbreviations

beg	begin, beginning	k	knit	sk	skip
CC	contrasting color	k 2 tog	knit 2 together	SKP	slip-knit-pass
ch	chain	lp	loop	sl	slip
circ	circular	MC	main color	sl st	slip stitch
cn	cable needle	mos	months	sp	space
dc	double crochet	no	number	st(s)	stitch(es)
dec	decrease(s), decreasing	oz	ounce(s)	St st	stockinette stitch
dp	double-point	p	purl	tbl	through back loop
foll	follows, following	pat	pattern	tog	together
gr	gram(s)	rem	remaining, remainder	tr	treble crochet
hdc	half double crochet	rep	repeat	yo	yarn over
hk	hook	rnd	round	mm	millimeters
inc	increase(s), increasing	sc	single crochet	cm	centimeters

Equivalency Charts

Inches and Metrics

Inches	MM	Inches	CM	Inches	CM	Inches	CM
⅛	3	4	10	10⅛	26	18½	47
¼	6	4¼	11	11	28	19¼	49
½	13	5	13	11¾	30	20	51
¾	20	5½	14	12¼	31	21¼	54
1¼	32	6	15	13	33	22	56
1½	38	6⅝	17	13¾	35	23¼	59
1¾	44	7	18	14¼	36	24¾	63
2	51	7¾	20	15¾	40	27½	70
3	76	8¼	21	16½	42	29¼	74
3½	90	9	23	17	43	31½	80
		9⅜	24	17¾	45	33	84
						35	89

Knitting Needles

American	Metric	English
1	2¾ mm	12
2	3 mm	11
3	3 mm	10
4	3¾ mm	9
5	4 mm	8
6	4½ mm	7
7	5 mm	6
8	5½ mm	5
9	6 mm	4
10	6½ mm	3
10½	7 mm	2
11	7½ mm	1

Crochet Hooks

American	Metric	English
B/1	2 mm	14
C/2	2½ mm	12/13
D/3	3 mm	11
E/4	3½ mm	9/10
F/5	4 mm	8
G/6	4½ mm	7
H/8	5 mm	6
H/8	5½ mm	5
I/9	6 mm	4
J/10	6½ mm	3
K	7 mm	2

Transferring Designs and Markings onto Fabric

Trace the design from the book or use the pattern piece you have enlarged. Then use one of the following methods.

1. Insert dressmaker's carbon between the pattern and the fabric and trace over the design with a pencil or tracing wheel.

2. For smooth, light-colored fabrics, turn your traced design over and retrace the lines on the wrong side of the paper with a soft lead pencil. Place the pattern right side up on the fabric and trace over the lines again. The pencil lines on the wrong side will come off on your fabric.

3. Trace the design using a marker or dark lead pencil. Place the fabric over the paper, taping it in place against a window—during daylight hours—or a light-box and trace the lines on the fabric.

4. To mark dots, darts, and other placement markings on the wrong side of fabric pieces, pin pattern to fabric and insert pin at marking. Lift up edge of pattern and mark fabric with lead or pastel pencil.

5. Use special transfer pens following manufacturer's directions.

How to Enlarge Patterns and Designs

When the pattern or design for project is larger than can be accommodated on the book's page, a scaled-down version is printed with a superimposed grid that looks like graph paper.

The instructional text and the legend on the grid will say, for example, "Each square = 1" (2.5cm)." This means, simply, that no matter what the size of the grid squares, each one represents one inch of actual size in the project. If the grid squares are ⅛" (3mm) and the legend reads, "Each square = 1" (2.5cm)," then the actual parts will be eight times larger than they appear in the patterns.

To make an enlargement of a gridded design or pattern with a specified enlargement scale, follow these steps:

1. Lay out your own graph paper or purchase some with the correct size larger grid squares.

2. Count the number of squares the smaller design covers from side to side and top to bottom, and mark off the same number of squares on the larger grid. Put dots at the corners of the rectangular area on the larger grid.

3. To enlarge the design, copy the pattern lines from the smaller grid to the larger grid, one square at a time. Use a ruler to transfer the straight lines and a French curve or a compass to reproduce curved lines. When all the lines are transferred, the enlarged pattern is ready to use.

4. If you are using an unusual grid size and plan to make a number of patterns, you will save time if you draw a master grid on heavy paper or use a single sheet of graph paper. Tape a layer of tracing paper over the grid and draw the pattern on it. When the pattern is complete, remove the tracing paper and save the grid to use again.

5. Patterns on grids can also be photostated to the scale given on the drawing. This process is somewhat expensive. Check your local Yellow Pages for a photostat service in your area.

Laundering, Cleaning and Blocking Hand-knitting and Crochet

Hand Washing

Wools, wool blends, and acrylics can be washed and rinsed by hand in lukewarm water. Use a mild soap. Gently squeeze suds and water through inside-out garment. Do not rub, wring, or twist. After rinsing, squeeze out as much water as possible. Lay garment flat on a towel and bunch into shape. Allow to dry completely.

Colorfast cottons (always test them, no matter what the label says) can be hand washed in the above manner. However, cotton knits hold so much water that the garment may take a very long time to dry, unless you employ some sort of centrifugal force, like the spin cycle of a washing machine. If you can't do this, it is better to dry clean cotton knits.

Machine Washing

We hope that when you shop for heirloom-making materials, you won't sacrifice quality for machine washability. There are, however, a number of nice-looking machine washable yarns available.

Some wools are machine washable but not machine dryable; acrylics usually wash and dry in the machine; some cottons and linens hold up very well in the machine. Follow the instructions on the label and test-wash a swatch first.

Dry Cleaning

Dry cleaning can be used on all natural fibers, but it will melt some acrylics. For silks and rayons, dry cleaning is the safest method, and it works well for cottons and wools. Tell your dry cleaner not to press the garments and not to put them on hangers, and they will come back to you in good shape.

Blocking

You may want to block a garment lightly before or after sewing it together. This step is not always necessary—slight irregularities are what makes handwork look like handwork. If your stitches are very uneven, a few washings will correct this more than blocking can.

To block, lay garment wrong side up on a padded surface. Dampen garment, bunch into shape; allow to dry completely. Or cover garment with a wet press cloth and steam lightly with a hot iron, taking care not to let the weight of the iron rest on the fabric. Do not steam or stretch ribbing—it will lose elasticity.

Laundering, Blocking and Framing Embroidery

Laundering

If the finished piece needs cleaning, wash it in cold water with mild soap. Handle it gently; rinse thoroughly. Roll it in a towel to remove excess moisture. Then iron it dry, covering the front of the work with a handkerchief. Iron mostly on the back.

Blocking

Blocking your needlework will give it a fresh, finished look and prepare it for framing. With the piece still in the embroidery frame, wet a clean cloth and lay it on the right side of the needlework. Remove the cloth when dry.

To block after washing

1. Mount a piece of heavy paper on a large board and draw the exact outside size of your work on the paper.

2. While the embroidered piece is still wet but not dripping, fasten it to the board at each corner and then at the center of each side with rust-proof push pins or thumb tacks.

3. Continue adding pins halfway between those already in place until you have placed pins no more than ½-in. apart all around the piece.

4. Allow the piece to dry completely.

Mounting and Framing

Whether you made your embroidery to fit a frame you already had or you purchased a new frame, it should be large enough to allow some plain background fabric to extend beyond the embroidered area. Traditionally, the fabric border is of equal width on the top and the sides but slightly wider at the bottom of the piece. But you can use your own judgement. Cut a piece of mat board to fit desired frame size; center the embroidery on the white side of the board and draw the excess fabric over it. If there is more than 1½ to 2 inches of extra fabric, trim it off.

Cross-Stitch Alphabet

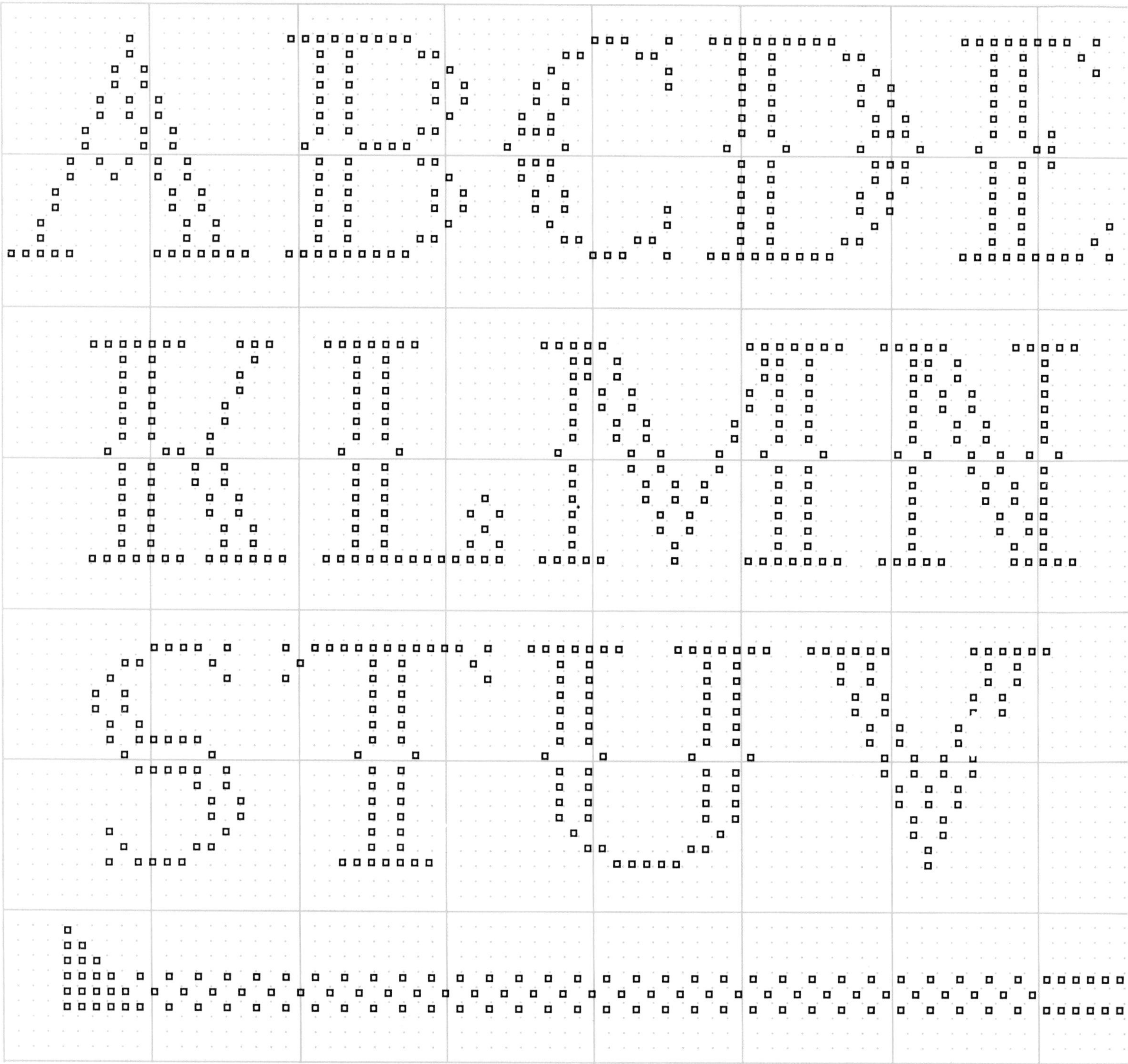

and Numbers Chart

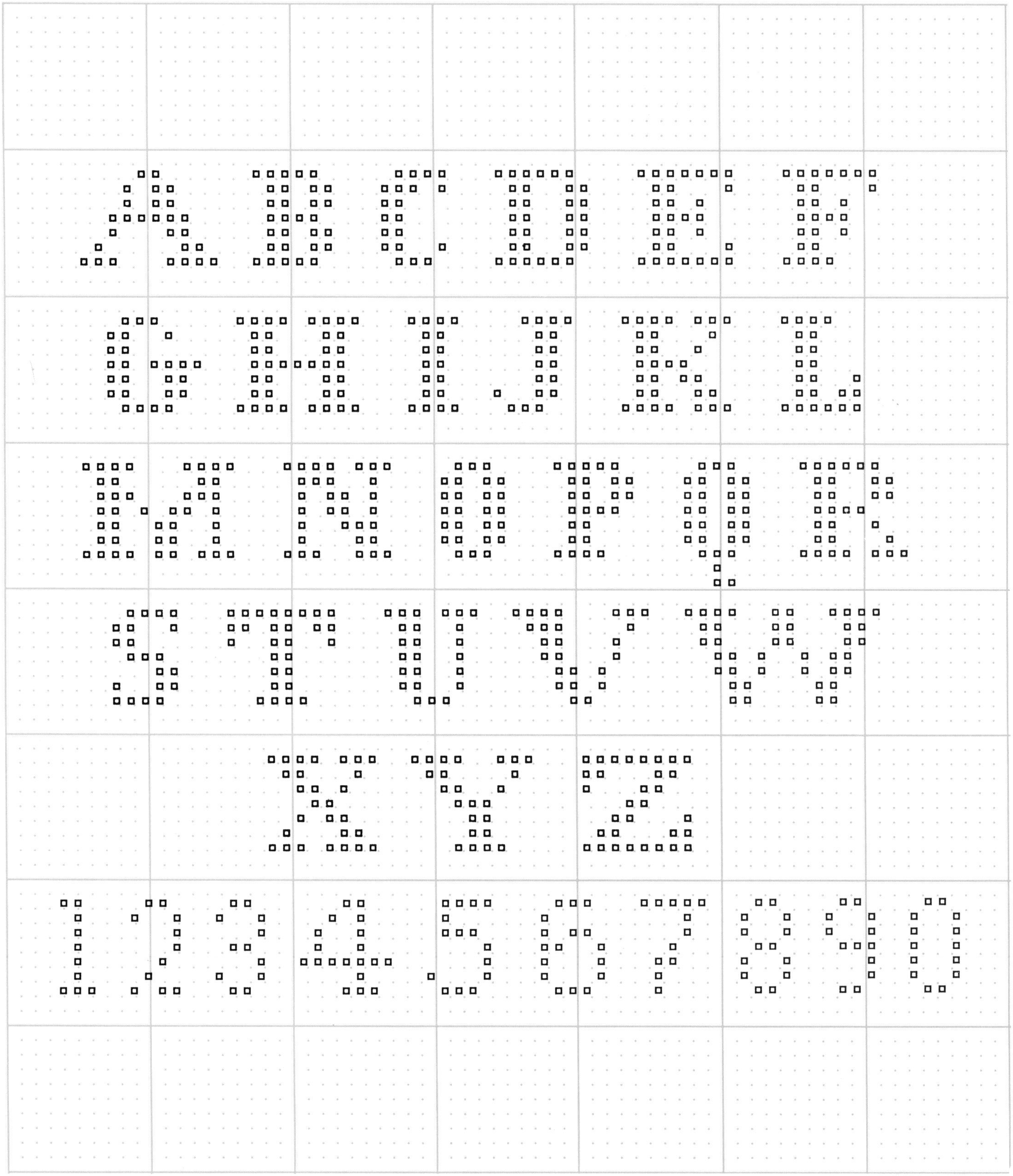
ABCDEF
GHIJKL
MNOPQR
STUVW
XYZ
1234567890

Baby Dolls

e asked Marsha Evans Moore to design some baby-sized dolls to model the garments for this book. As you can see from the photographs, she produced some beautiful little creatures, in newborn and 6 months sizes. They are of simple, squarish construction, with embroidered features, and we are so pleased with them that we have included the instructions in the book.

Perhaps one of these dolls can serve as a durable playmate for the flesh-and-blood babies in your life, or, perhaps, as models for the beautiful garments you make from this book that the child has (alas, all too quickly) outgrown.

The making of a doll allows for aesthetic intervention that is quite impossible with real babies. You can select skin, eye, and hair color, and make the hair straight or curly. A pretty ribbon bow is enough to transform a little boy doll into a little girl doll.

Shop for these items

45" wide muslin or cotton fabric, desired color.
⅝ yd for newborn-size doll.
¾ yd for 6 months size doll.
Worsted-weight cotton yarn, 1¾ oz. (50 gr) skein, desired color for hair.
Six-strand embroidery floss, 1 skein each black, white, pink, light brown, and 1 skein desired eye color.
Cotton sewing thread to match fabric and yarn.
Polyester fiberfill.
Dressmaker's carbon paper.
Tissue or tracing paper (to make paper pattern).
4 sheets 8½ x 11" paper (to make curly hair).

Cutting and marking the fabric

Enlarge and trace pattern pieces, transferring all markings. Cut out paper pattern and arrange on folded fabric. Cut 2 bodies, 2 heads, 4 ears, 4 arms, and 4 legs. Transfer dots to wrong side of fabric and small broken lines to right side. For head, transfer feature markings to right side of front head piece and broken line to right side of head back.

Putting the pieces together

1. With right sides in, stitch ears together in pairs along outer curve. Trim and clip seam allowance along stitching. Turn right side out. Stuff ear with small amount of stuffing. Baste along inner curve. Quilt along broken lines.

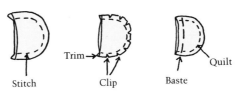

2. Baste ears to head front between dots. Stitch heads together leaving lower edge open. Clip seam allowance. Turn right side out. Stuff head firmly.

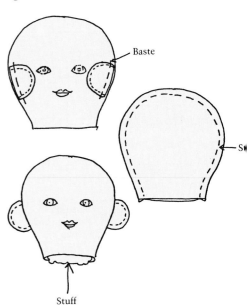

3. With right sides in, stitch bodies together along shoulders and sides below dots. Clip curves along shoulder seam. Turn right side out. Turn under ¼" along neck edge and armhole openings; baste edge in place. Insert head in neck opening, matching seams at sides; slip-stitch body to head.

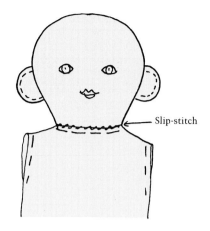

Slip-stitch

5. Right sides in, stitch legs to lower edge of body between dots. Stuff body. Turn in seams to line to form a pleat. Slip-stitch lower edge of back to legs and front.

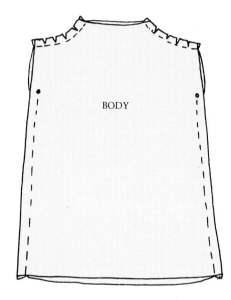

BODY

4. With right sides in, stitch legs together in pairs, leaving top edge open. Clip seam allowance along curves. Turn right side out. Stuff foot to line. Tuck in seams to vertical line to form a pleat on each side; stitch across broken line. Stuff lower leg; pleat and stitch across line in same manner. Stuff upper leg; baste along top.

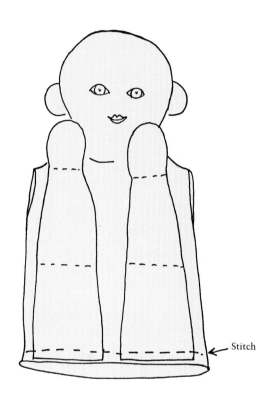

Stitch

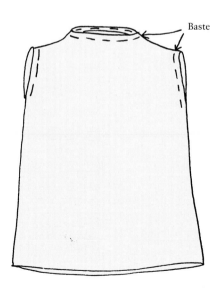

Baste

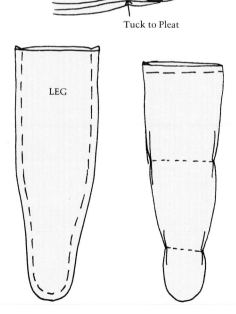

LEG

Tuck to Pleat

LEG

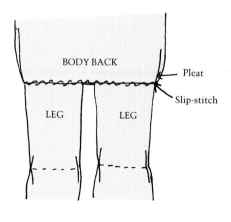

BODY BACK

Pleat

Slip-stitch

LEG   LEG

6. With right sides in, stitch arms together in pairs, leaving straight end open. Clip seam allowance along curves; trim to ⅛" along hand. Turn right side out; stuff lower arm to line. Tuck in seam to form pleat and stitch along line. Stuff upper arm; baste along end. Insert end in opening of body matching dots. Slip-stitch along front and back.

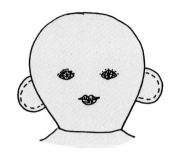

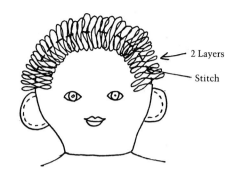

2 Layers

Stitch

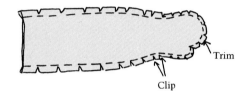

ARM

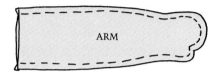

Trim

Clip

7. Embroider sections of eyes and mouth with satin stitch. Embroider brows and lash line with stem stitch.

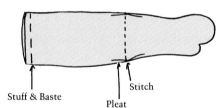

Stuff & Baste

Pleat

Stitch

8. For curly hair, fold paper in quarters lengthwise. Fold 3 sheets for small dolls and 4 for large dolls. Wind yarn closely around strips crosswise to form loops. Using matching thread, stitch lengthwise down center of strip through paper and yarn. Tear paper from looped yarn along perforation formed by stitching. Pin 2 layers of looped yarn across top of head and remaining strips to back of head above broken line spiraling to center. Sew in place along machine stitching line with running stitches.

Stitch

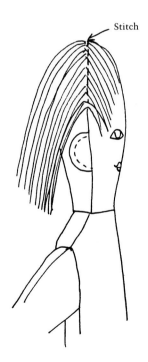

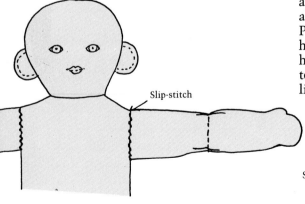

Slip-stitch

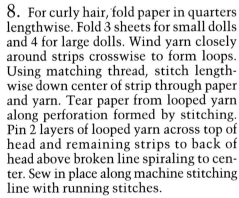

Stitch

Yarn

9. For straight hair, cut strands of yarn 10″ long. Lay strands close together up back of head, running from 1″ below broken line at nape of neck past seam at top of head. With matching sewing thread, backstitch strands down a few, at a time along seam at top of head, and along broken line at nape of neck. Trim ends evenly. For ponytail, cut strands of yarn 12″ long. Center these over seam at top center of head; sew in place with backstitch. Pull ponytail ends up away from head. Tie a ribbon bow around ponytail.

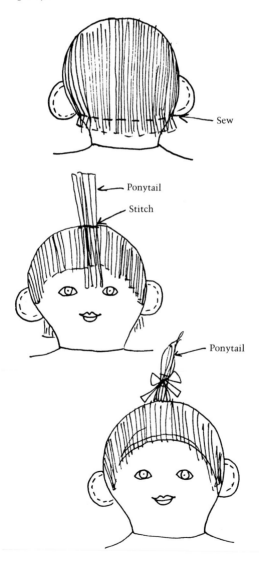

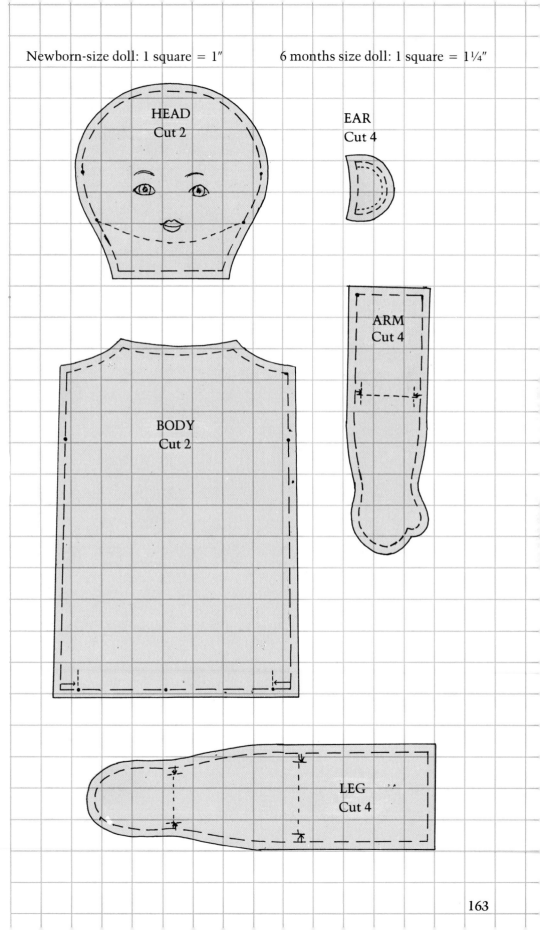

Newborn-size doll: 1 square = 1″   6 months size doll: 1 square = 1¼″

HEAD
Cut 2

EAR
Cut 4

ARM
Cut 4

BODY
Cut 2

LEG
Cut 4

Sew

Ponytail

Stitch

Ponytail

Ribbon Rose Hangers

You may have noticed the satin, padded hangers in some of the photographs. There is one on the cover photo. These were specially made up for us and this is how the hangers, and the little ribbon roses, are made.

Shop for these items

Purchased satin-covered hanger.
Single-face satin ribbons in colors desired in ⅜" and ⅝" widths to make about 12 roses, plus ¼ yd. ⅜" green ribbon for bow.
Thread to match ribbons.
Sewing needle; yarn needle or thin knitting needle.

To make hangers

Remove ribbon from center of hanger. Pick out stitches at center and remove satin cover from each arm of hanger. Cut about 2" from each end of hanger to make size hanger desired. Trim satin cover at center edges to fit size of hanger. Cut off excess padding. Slip satin cover back onto hanger; turn in raw edge and slip-stitch at center.

To make roses

Thread needle and knot single end of thread. Cut ribbon in 4-to-6 inch lengths. To form center, roll one end of ribbon over yarn needle or knitting needle 6 turns to make a tight tube. Tack at base to secure. To form petals, fold top edge of unwound ribbon downward toward you so top edge is parallel to tube and folded edge is at a 45 degree angle. Roll tube across fold loosely at top and tightly at base; tack. Continue to fold, roll and tack until rose is desired size. The finished size depends on the width of ribbon. Tight winding makes buds, looser folds make full-blown roses. To finish, turn under raw edge and sew to base. Sew roses to ribbon at center of hanger. Add bow.

Ribbon Rose Hangers

To form the center, roll one end of ribbon six turns to make a tight tube. Sew a few stitches at base to secure.

To form petals, fold top edge of unwound ribbon downward and toward you so it is parallel to tube and folded edge is at a 45° angle.

Roll tube across fold, loosely at top and tightly at base. Tack.

Continue to fold, roll and tack, shaping the rose as you work, until it is desired size. Finish by turning under raw edge and sewing to base. Sew in place.

To make a bouquet, slip a long piece of fine wire through the stitches; wind it around the base of the rose a few times and straighten for stem.

Name _____   Date of Birth _____

Place of Birth _____   Time of Birth _____

Zodiac Sign _____

Age	Height	Weight	Hair & Eye Color	New Words	New Friends	New Foods	New Accomplishments

Index